SL740-AG-RPT-010

0910-LP-115-1677

U.S. NAVY SALVAGE REPORT USNS SGT MATEJ KOCAK (T-AK 3005) SALVAGE AND TEMPORARY REPAIRS

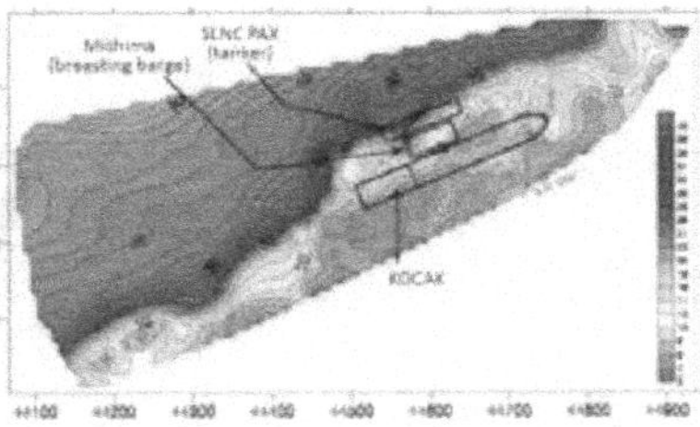

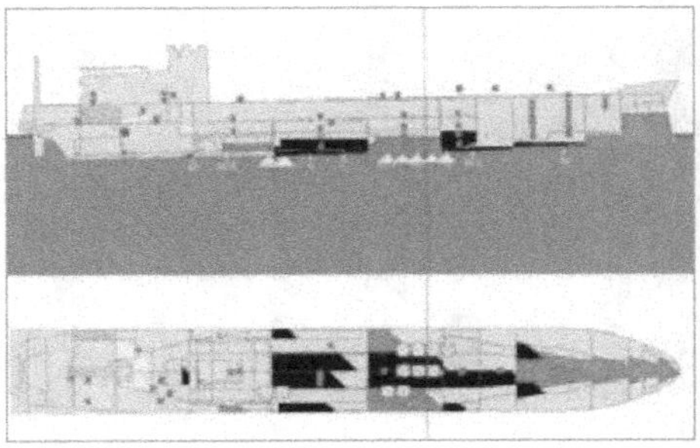

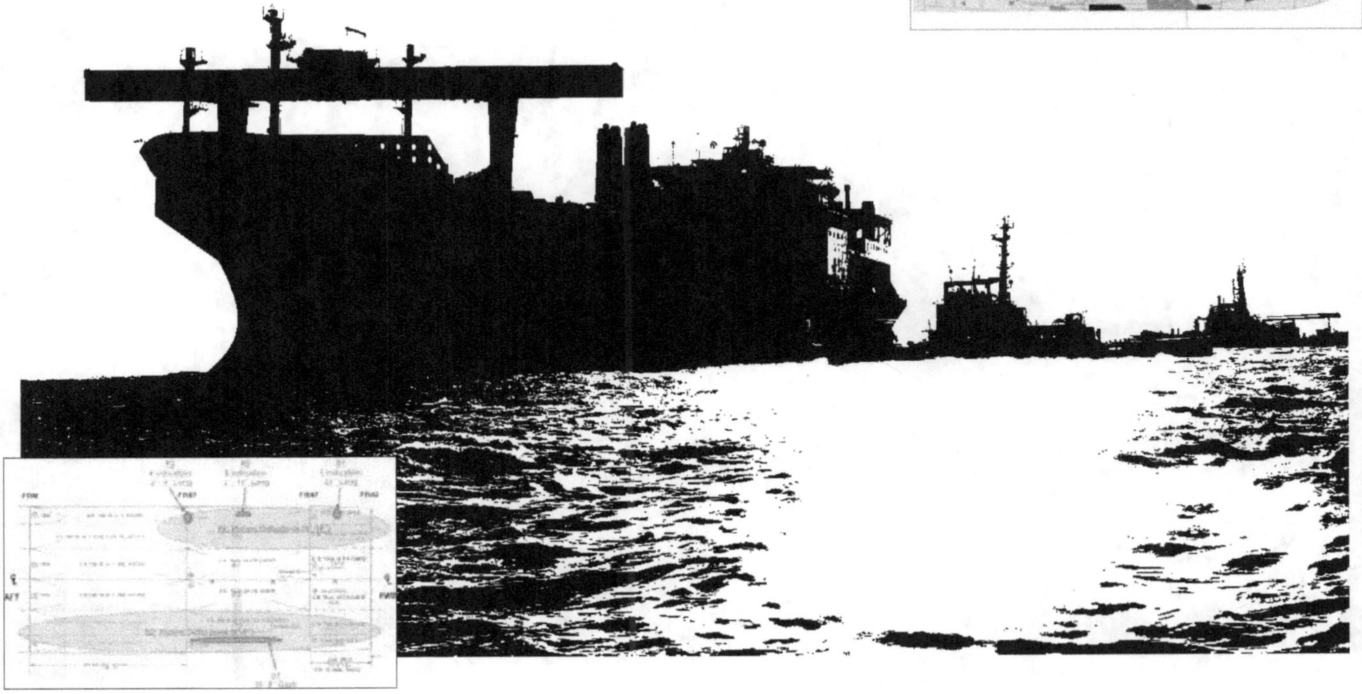

Distribution Statement A: This document has been approved for public release and sale, its distribution is unlimited.

Published by Direction of Commander, Naval Sea Systems Command

May 2015

FOREWORD

The grounding of USNS SGT MATEJ KOCAK (T-AK 3005) could have been a disaster for the U.S. Navy. KOCAK held, in its Cargo Holds, significant and costly material which had been loaded for transport to support Exercise COBRA GOLD scheduled to take place in Thailand later that spring. Loss of that cargo due to flooding and hull damage would have been very costly. She also stored over 700,000 gallons of marine diesel and JP5 within her fuel tanks which, if spilled, would have been a huge disaster for the pristine Eastern shore of Okinawa, Japan.

Fortunately, the worst case disaster did not occur. This was the result of a number of factors. The salvors encountered favorable winds and only moderate seas during the period the ship was aground. Additionally, the ship was well protected from southwesterly through northeasterly winds and at no time did the wind and seas combine to cause follow-on hull damage. But the salvors made their own good fortune as well. Our success could be credited to the following actions:

- SUPSALV's seasoned Western Pacific Salvage Contractor, SMIT Singapore, was ready and capable of meeting the needs of this job.
- SUPSALV's Naval Architect was well versed with our Program of Ship Salvage Engineering (POSSE) and could precisely model the ship and assess what condition would be needed to refloat the ship.
- Military Sealift Command, the operator of KOCAK, was an active and willing partner in the salvage task and managed timely and proactive support for the salvage effort.
- Despite hitting the reef at speed, KOCAK was not badly damaged during the initial grounding. While holed both port and starboard, the innerbottom ballast and fuel tank tops were largely holding and preventing massive flooding.
- USS BONHOMME RICHARD's damage control team's arrival on 27 January came at a time when the salvors had not yet ramped up to their full strength. The Navy repair party was capable, spirited, and well organized. Their impact was immediate and significant. KOCAK's undamaged cargo is the result.

Added to the salvage success was the professionalism of the repair team that SUPSALV's Underwater Ship Husbandry division managed which restored the seaworthiness of USNS KOCAK. Phoenix, International, our undersea operations contractor, knows their business and executed the repair plan without delay, obtaining ABS and USCG approval of their accomplishments.

Our success was truly a team effort and the result of years of training and preparation. The results were commendable.

Gregg. W. Baumann
Captain, USN
Director of Ocean Engineering
Supervisor of Salvage and Diving

This page intentionally left blank.

Table of Contents

List of Figures

List of Tables

Attachments:

A. Liquid Offload Plan

B. Refloat Schedule

C. Environmental Response Plan

D. POSSE Report

E. USNS STG MATEJ KOCAK Emergent Repair Plan

F. Environmental Damage Assessment

G. Phoenix Completion Report

This page intentionally left blank.

1. Introduction and Background

This salvage report documents the recovery and temporary repairs conducted by NAVSEA 00C, Supervisor of Salvage and Diving, for the Military Sealift Command. The operations took place off the east coast of Okinawa from 22 January 2015, the date of the grounding, to 20 February 2015, when the temporary repairs were completed. Details of the efforts and accomplishments are provided in this report.

1-1. KOCAK Grounding Details and Initial Events

While underway outbound from White Beach, Okinawa, Maritime Prepositioning Ship USNS SGT MATEJ KOCAK (T-AK 3005) grounded on a reef in vicinity of buoy #1 at approximately 1110 local time on 22 January 2015. The ship was underway enroute to Thailand following ammunition on load to support Exercise COBRA GOLD. Approximately 91 personnel were on board to support this exercise.

Figure 1-1. USNS KOCAK grounded on Ufubishi Reef, Okinawa, Japan. Reef shoal is marked by breaking waves in the foreground.

The ship had been loaded with U.S. Army and U.S. Marine Corps hardware at U.S. Navy Commander Fleet Activities Okinawa (CFAO) White Beach and departed the pier at 0600 that morning with a pilot and two tugs. After anchoring in anchorage W4 and discharging the pilot, the ship weighed anchor and proceeded to sea. When the ship hit the reef, the ship's heading was approximately 066 degrees. Two tugs that reported to the scene were used to maintain the position of the ship's stern preventing damage to the ship's running gear or hull aft of the ground contact points. The vessel reported multiple penetrations on her starboard side and took on a port list of approximately 1.5 degrees but remained stable. There were no personnel injuries and no oil in the water in the vicinity of the ship. Japanese Coast Guard was notified. Figure 1-2 shows the location of the grounding site and route the ship intended to travel.

1-1.1. Updated Ship Conditions

By 23 January, KOCAK's Master reported that the lower Cargo Hold 3A (tank top level) seawater level had increased to approximately 12 inches, currently at "Humvee tire level". Flooding boundaries had been set and dewatering equipment was in use. The ship remained stable and firmly on the reef forward. The stern (including propeller and rudder) remain clear of the bottom with the assistance of a tug.

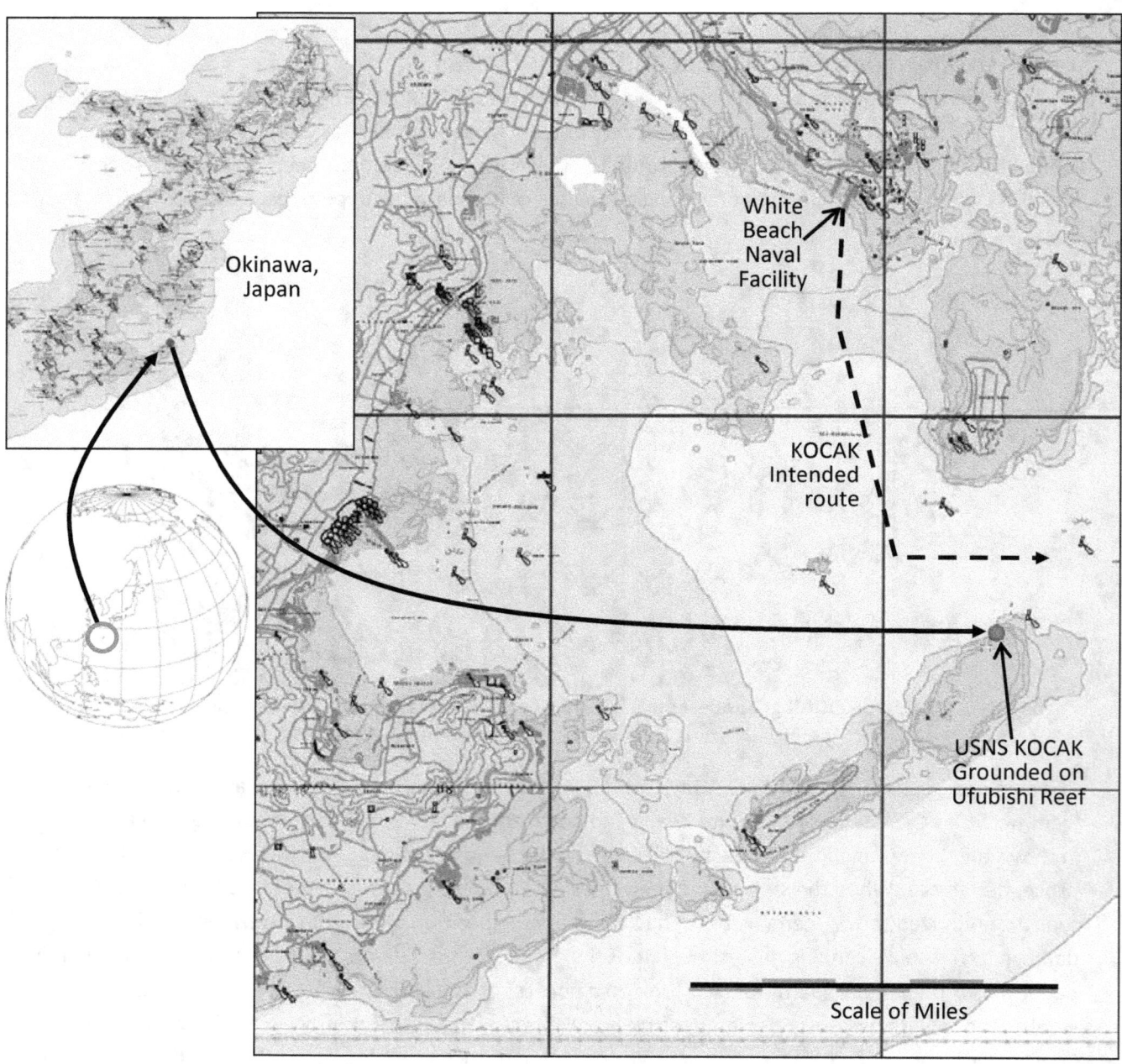

Figure 1-2. Location map for Okinawa, Japan, Nakagusuku Bay, and USNS KOCAK grounding.

Later that day (23 January) the floodwater reached and ignited an unsecured battery in one of the cargo vehicles. The fire was extinguished and the hold secured. Over the next three days the floodwater in Cargo Hold 3A rose to a level of approximately 6-ft which is below the waterline and indicated a slow leak rather than complete free communication. The lower deck watertight vehicle doors on the port side between Cargo Holds 3A and 4 and Cargo Holds 4 and 4A had been forced out of alignment and were no longer tight. The gaps were plugged and communication from the flooded Cargo Hold 3A was reduced to a manageable level. Additionally, minor deflections in the deck and bulkhead between Cargo Holds 4 and 4A both port and starboard were reported.

1-2. Purpose of Report

This report has been prepared to document the techniques and procedures used during this successful refloating operation and capture any lessons learned that can applied to future operations. This incident is one where the salvage operations were immediately followed by hull repair tasks. SUPSALV, with its regional salvage contract and its diving services contract had the ability to select from a range of capabilities in support of MSC's grounded ship.

1-3. SUPSALV Tasking and Scope of Mission

Following the grounding, immediate coordination between MSC and SUPSALV began. A draft message was forwarded to Mr. Michael Herb, Salvage Division Head, on 22 January and verbal approval from CNO OPN31 was received the same day. These unofficial communications were followed up on 24 January where, via Navy message, COMSC requested U.S. Navy salvage assistance in support of USNS SGT MATEJ KOCAK. MSC, citing OPNAVINST 4740.2G, the Navy's Salvage Program[1], requested SUPSALV provide salvage services "to assess, plan, and execute refloating operations for USNS SGT MATEJ KOCAK". They indicated the desired end state was the refloating / recovery of KOCAK for safe transit to an acceptable repair facility and requested immediate mobilization of a salvage unit for recovery of KOCAK. CNO, in following the verbal approval, approved MSC's official message request for assistance on 27 January.

Based on the 22 January verbal authorization, SUPSALV authorized their Western Pacific Salvage Contractor, SMIT, based in Singapore, to provide a team, led by a seasoned Salvage Master, to assess the situation onboard KOCAK. SUPSALV and a Naval Architect from the Salvage Division had also deployed and began working on a debeaching solution. The near immediate SUPSALV response in tasking SMIT was based on MSC's verbal request and CNO's verbal authorization. In-house funds were used to begin the initial salvage assessment but actual MSC funding for $2,450,000 was received on 23 January allowing SUPSALV to ramp up the SMIT support and add Nippon Salvage (SMIT's Japanese subcontractor) manpower and equipment.

With a salvage plan developed and KOCAK's debeaching scheduled, the need to perform emergency repairs was evident. SUPSALV proposed to MSC that SUPSALV use some of the funds MSC had provided

---

[1] OPNAV Instruction 4740.2G provides implementation policy for salvage and recovery operations involving U.S. government ships, cargo, aircraft, and other objects, such as space vehicles, nose cones, and weapons. It specifies that when needed salvage and recovery assistance exceeds organic fleet capabilities, TYCOMs should request services of COMNAVSEASYSCOM (00C) via CNO.

for salvage operations to accomplish the repairs. When MSC agreed, and on 27 January, G+5 days, $600K was pulled from SMIT's delivery order and used to task Phoenix International to provide emergency ship repair services for KOCAK.

1-4. Operational Considerations

No salvage operation is performed in a vacuum. Every ship and environment combine to form a unique situation. This operation, conducted off the east coast of Okinawa Island had its share of individual characteristics that needed to be considered in order to successfully complete the tasks. This is a listing of the more significant ones.

1-4.1. Cargo

USNS SGT MATEJ KOCAK (T-AK 3005) ran aground after loading cargo to support operation COBRA GOLD which was to take place in Thailand beginning in February 2015. The cargo on board consisted of vehicles, helicopters, trailers, shipping containers, and ammunition. Combined cargo weight was 3,817 long tons. The cargo on deck and in the holds was a factor in the stability calculations. Discrepancies were found between the actual total weight and location of the cargo loads and the reported weight and centers. SUPSALV's Program of Ship Salvage Engineering (POSSE) was used to consolidate cargo weight details into individual point loads which assisted in accurately modeling the ship's actual loaded condition. Two additional notes about the cargo: The cargo in the hold number 3 was immersed to greater than 6 feet and a battery fire from one of the vehicles in that hold resulted in toxic atmosphere in Hold 3A which prevented free access to the space for a couple of days.

1-4.2. Liquid

In order to ensure an accurate starting point for developing a refloating plan for USNS KOCAK, the weight and location of all liquid cargo and bunkers needed to be incorporated into POSSE software. The tanks were manually sounded and compared to the engine room tank level indicators. This gave an indication of which Tank Level Indicators (TLIs) were not accurate. When USNS KOCAK grounded, she was carrying 658,468 gallons (15,680 bls) of diesel fuel marine (DFM) and 92,290 gallons (2197 bls) of JP5. In order to lighten the ship for refloating, 11,000 barrels of DFM were pumped off on 2 February, 11 days after KOCAK's grounding (G+11). Additionally, water (mixed with trace oil) was pumped from holds 3, 4 and 4A. This oily waste was pumped into KOCAK's waste tanks and then to the U.S. Navy Command Fleet Activity Okinawa (U.S. CAFO) waste oil containment barges weather permitting. Lastly, ballast tanks were pumped down to refloat the ship. The liquid offload plan, Attachment A, identifies the tanks that were emptied to reduce ground reaction to zero.

1-4.3. On Deck

The cargo on deck also presented some stability challenges to the salvage crews. This cargo included 2 Chinook helicopters, a number of heavy trucks and trailers, and containers. The Naval Architects had to be mindful of their location high up on the ship when planning the fuel offload and deballasting as they were reducing weight concentrated low in the ship (pumping down fuel and ballast tanks) and not reducing weight in the Cargo Holds and on deck.

1-4.4. Weather

The salvage team was fortunate to encounter above average temperatures and no major storms during the time USNS KOCAK was aground. Moderate winds did limit the time the waste containment barges could be alongside KOCAK. The actual liquid offload required moderately calm conditions to allow KOCAK to moor with Nippon's salvage barge, Mishima, and the tanker, SLNC PAX, for the 10-11 hours needed to offload DFM and JP5. The extraction, which took place on 3 February (G+12), was timed to coincide with above average high tide which occurred at the end of the day.

1-4.5. Operator Responsibilities

Keystone Shipping Company headquartered just north of Philadelphia, (http://www.keyship.com) holds the contract with MSC to operate the USNS SGT MATEJ KOCAK (T-AK 3005). Their mariners were operating the ship when she ran aground. Keystone took responsibility for the Environmental Response planning and their Port Engineer coordinated repair efforts between SUPSALV's repair team and KOCAK's ships force, Keystone HQ, and USCG/ABS certification authority.

1-4.6. Safety

Safety was the primary consideration in every aspect of the operation with environmental protection immediately following. Small boat operations were restricted to periods of daylight. On the days where the sea state had risen, embarkation on KOCAK became difficult using the Jacobs Ladder. Extreme care was required.   Fortunately the weather cooperated for the most part allowing for safe operations.

1-4.7. Environmental Response Planning and Reef Restoration

The ship's operator, Keystone, through ECM Maritime Services, who are under Keystone contract to provide OPA 90 services to all of Keystone's fleet, contracted with Marentas to develop a Pollution Prevention Contingency Plan for the USNS KOCAK grounding incident. Marentas, who is based in the Far-East, selected the local oil spill response organization (OSRO) Maritime Disaster Prevention Center (MDPC) who had store of equipment and personnel on staff on the shore of Nakagusuku Bay to provide response capability and services during the fuel offload and extraction.

U.S. Navy Commander Fleet Activities Okinawa (CFAO) White Beach port services supported the operation's environmental response by provision of the waste oil containment barges and also by establishing a perimeter boom around USNS KOCAK once the ship was returned to the pier.

Naval Facilities (NAVFAC) Engineering and Expeditionary Warfare Center's (EXWC) Marine Resource Assessment Diving Services (MRADS) provided an Environmental Engineer to assist MSC in assessing the ecological impact of the grounding and extent of the reef damage.

This page intentionally left blank.

2. Overview of Operations

SUPSALV's response to USNS SGT MATEJ KOCAK (T-AK 3005) grounding could be divided into three phases. The first phase was discovery, where tasking and assessment took place. Blue shading in the calendar below identifies the discovery phase. The second was the salvage phase where damage control, weight reduction and refloating took place (pink highlights) and the third was the conduct of temporary repairs (green shading). Additional actions took place during these phases, including development of an environmental response plan, ammunition and cargo offload, and environmental damage assessment but this report will focus on SUPSALV actions and accomplishments. The major events of the salvage and repair operations are provided in Table 2-1. A detailed summary of events between January 31 and 3 February is provided at the Refloat Schedule in Attachment B.

Table 2-1. Major Operational Milestones

Sunday	Monday	Tuesday	Wednesday	Thursday	Friday	Saturday
Blue shading represents the Discovery phase. Pink shading represents the Salvage phase Green shading represents the Temporary Repair phase.				**Jan 22** • 1100 KOCAK reports grounding • 00C receives verbal authority to salvage	**23** • SMIT / Nippon mobilize assessment team • 00C and 00C24 depart DC	**24** • SMIT Nippon board KOCAK to begin assessment
25 • 00CL departs DC for Okinawa • Army Special Forces Team conduct dive survey	**26** • Phoenix tasked to provide UWSH repairs	**27** • USS Bonhomme Richard DC team arrives • SMIT/Nippon increase size of salvage teams	**28** • Mishima placed on hire • Salvage/DC teams stabilize casualty	**29** • 00C distributes Rev 1 of refloat plan	**30** • Nippon conducts salvage dive survey	**31** • Mishima at White Beach pier collecting hoses and fenders • Environmental Prevention plan issued
Feb 1 • SLNC PAX arrives White Beach	**2** • Defueling operations conducted	**3** • Deballasting & refloating operations • KOCAK back at White Beach pier by evening	**4** • Nippon salvage dive survey (at pier) • SUPSALV UWSH repair team arrives	**5** • UWSH team sets up dive site • AMMO Offload begins	**6** • 00C UWSH repair dive survey	**7** • 00C UWSH repair dive survey • Reef survey conducted
8 • General Cargo offload • UWSH Repairs commence	**9** • Helicopters removed from stern ramp onto Mishima	**10** • Reef survey conducted	**11** • Reef survey conducted	**12**	**13** • Repair Plan issued	**14**
15	**16** • Completed shell plate welds	**17**	**18**	**19** • All tanks isolated from holds	**20** • Cargo doors sealed – Repairs complete	

2-1. Command and Organization

As the grounding was reported via the Pentagon Battle Watch, COMPACFLT and COM7THFLT took an immediate interest in the proceedings. MSC ships assigned as preposition ships are under operational control of United States Transportation Command (USTRANSCOM). With command and control of USNS KOCAK, TRANSCOM assigned incident operational control (OPCON) to MSC with the direction to keep PACFLT and SEVENTHFLT informed.

This simplified the command structure. MSC Chief of Staff was on site and formed a team that incorporated expertise from a full range of players. The organization was a matrix vice stove piped organization and it worked well. While command and control remained with MSC, the individual team members worked with their counterparts to provide the best, coordinated service and solutions.

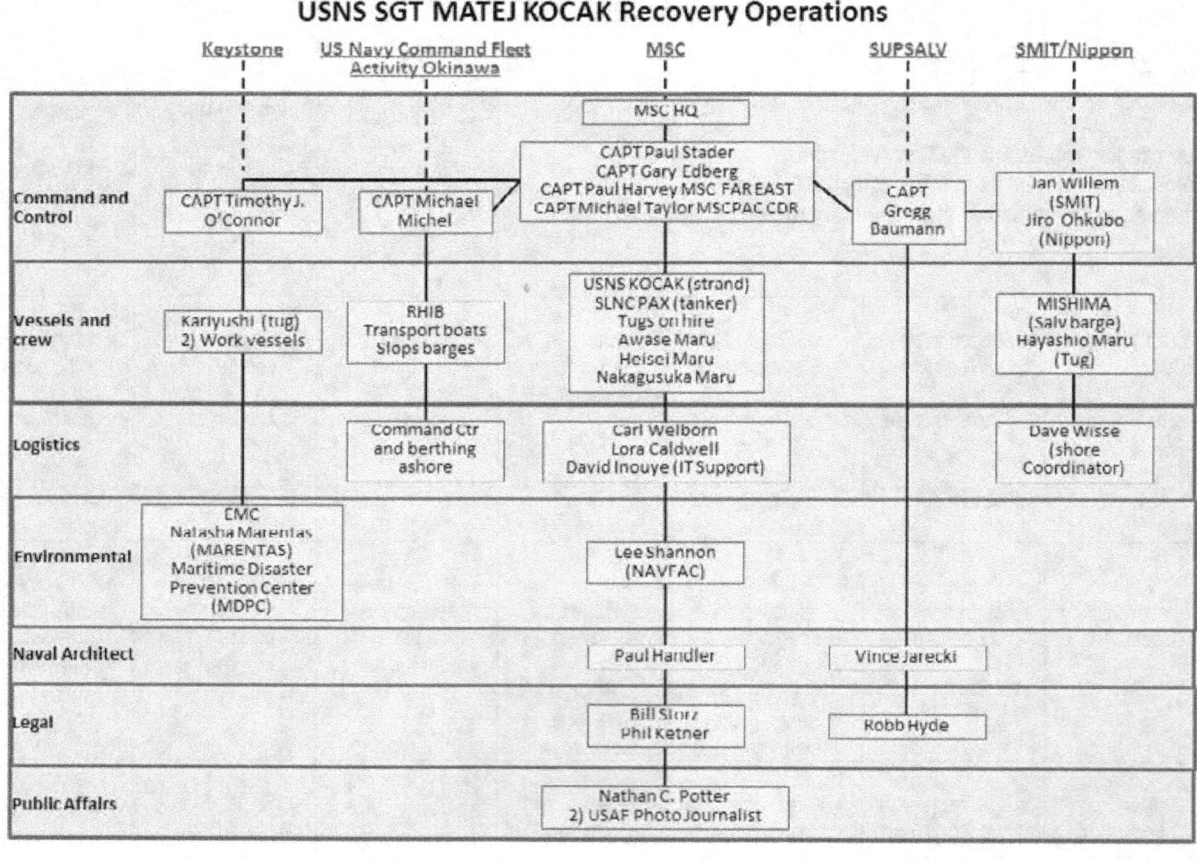

Figure 2-1. Recovery Organization

2-1.1. MSC

Military Sealift Command (MSC) is the owner of USNS SGT MATEJ KOCAK (T-AK 3005) and reports to TRANSCOM who has Operational Command of the vessel. MSC responded immediately to the news of the grounding with the provision of tug services and establishment of on-station support with a MSC Flyaway Team. MSC notified Japanese Coast Guard, Okinawa Defense Bureau and other Japanese federal and local government organizations. They also coordinated with CFAO to obtain space at White

Beach for housing and operations center space. MSC Battle Watch continued to monitor the salvage team's actions throughout the operation. MSC also directed the oil tanker, SLNC PAX, to report to Okinawa to take on fuel from KOCAK.

2-1.2. SUPSALV
Received notification and tasking from MSC on 22 January and issued verbal task orders to SMIT on 23 January. SUPSALV (00C) and SUPSALV's Naval Architect (00C24) departed Washington, D.C. on January 23 and arrived in Okinawa on January 24 to take charge of the salvage efforts. SUPSALV was tasked to support MSC to refloat USNS KOCAK. SUPSALV also provided a welding services team to conduct temporary repairs to allow USNS KOCAK to sail to a drydock facility for permanent repairs.

2-1.3. NAVSEA HQ
NAVSEA stood up SEA 05 Command Center at the Washington Navy Yard and participated in 0800 (East Coast) 2200 (JST) conference calls. SEA 05 engineers from Structures and Stability codes provided engineering support where needed.

2-1.4. COMPACFLT
Overall Fleet Commander. Dispatched the Pacific Fleet Salvage Officer who reported to KOCAK and supported salvage response throughout the operation.

2-1.5. Keystone Shipping Company
Keystone is the operating company for USNS KOCAK under contract with MSC. Keystone deployed a Fleet Safety, Quality Assurance Officer and Port Engineer to the ship to coordinate salvage and repair response. Keystone initiated contact with EMC Maritime Services to provide environmental response to the incident. EMC contracted with Maritime Disaster Prevention Center (MDPC) for a response coordinator.

2-1.6. SMIT and Nippon
SMIT holds the SUPSALV Western Pacific salvage contract and is available for tasking through that established contract. SMIT received verbal tasking on 23 January and immediately sent a Salvage Assessment Team and contracted for local salvage support from Nippon who had vessels and salvors in Japan. Both SMIT and NIPPON teams arrived at the Port of Naha during the afternoon of 23 January and met with MSC Director Carl Welborn to begin coordinating the salvage assessment. SMIT and Nippon teamed to provide salvors and equipment to support the operation.

2-1.7. U.S. Army
An 11-man Army SFG dive team conducted a dive survey on 25 January. Army LCU facilitated getting KOCAK military personnel off the ship. The LCU also supported environmental assessment after the vessel was refloated.

2-1.8. Japanese Coast Guard
The Japanese Coast Guard was very concerned with the potential for oil spilling from the KOCAK. MSC Public Affairs established channels of communication to ensure JCG was kept informed of the evolving situation. The JCG monitored the actions of the salvage team daily. At 1800 each day, a senior

representative attended a meeting at the command center and received a debriefing from MSC Chief of Staff and SUPSALV. A CFAO interpreter was used to facilitate communications. They also stationed vessels at the salvage site during the liquid offloading and retraction.

Figure 2-2. Japanese Coast Guard Briefing on 30 January where SUPSALV's Naval Architect, Vince Jarecki, briefed the Liquid Offload Plan to the assembled team.

2-2. Tasking and Funding

The NAVSEA Watch Officer received word from SEA 21 of the OPREP-3NB that had been issued by the Pentagon Battle Watch Captain on 22 January. That OPREP was forwarded to senior NAVSEA leadership and Mr. Michael Dean, SEA 00CB.

The official request for assistance came from COMSC message, dtg 240445Z JAN 15, to CNO requesting salvage assistance ISO USNS SGT MATEJ KOCAK. They requested SUPSALV "assess, plan, and execute refloating operations". This message arrived 2 days after MSC verbally requested NAVSEA for assistance.

SUPSALV issued a verbal order to SMIT on 22 January for $50,000 to provide for a Salvage Master and two support personnel to conduct assessment and planning operations in support of KOCAK grounding. As the scope of the operation expanded, that tasking grew to $2.5M to provide for emergency response and recovery operations for the USNS KOCAK grounding east of Okinawa, Japan. On 27 January, SUPSALV decreased SMIT's tasking from $2,450,000 to $1,850,000 in order to fund the Diving Services contract to support temporary hull repairs.

On 27 January, Phoenix was tasked to provide temporary repair services to USNS KOCAK. $600,000 was placed on the Delivery Order for immediate mobilization of personnel and equipment to conduct repair operations.

2-3. Mobilization

USNS KOCAK ran aground conveniently close to a U.S. Naval Station, U.S. Navy Commander Fleet Activities Okinawa (CFAO) White Beach, but inconveniently, thousands of miles from MSC and SUPSALV's home offices on the east coast of the United States. The total transit time from Washington, D.C. to Okinawa and on to White Beach was approximately 24 hours. SUPSALV's Western Pacific salvage contractor, SMIT is based in Singapore, and was able to quickly make the trip to the site of the grounding. Materials for repairs, which included steel that required mill test certificates and ABS approval had to be shipped from the United States and the ABS Inspector (who approved the repair plan) and Marine Chemist (who provided the Gas Free certificates needed for compartment welding) came from Tokyo to the site to support KOCAK repairs.

2-3.1. SUPSALV

NAVSEA Supervisor of Salvage (SUPSALV) and SEA 00C24 (SUPSALV Naval Architect) deployed on 23 January and arrived at White Beach late PM on 24 January after an approximate 24 hour total transit time. SUPSALV deployed their Admiralty Attorney on 25 January to assist MSC in defining and differentiating the owner and operator responsibilities and ensuring SUPSALV wouldn't assume responsibility in areas that the operator should. SUPSALV also deployed one of its headquarters technical, professional and administrative support services contractors, ROH, Incorporated, to provide administrative support and to collect documentation to build a detailed salvage report.

2-3.2. SMIT

SMIT mobilized 23 January following verbal SUPSALV tasking. SMIT holds SUPSALV's Western Pacific Salvage Contract and is available for tasking via Delivery Order. The task specified that SMIT support shall include personnel, vessels, and equipment required for assessment, planning, stabilization, oil removal, and vessel recovery. Immediate contractor response was required to mitigate possible pollution risks, stabilize vessel and conduct refloating operations to prevent further environmental damage and damage to the vessel.

SMIT responded by sending a team of three, including a salvage master and salvage supervisor to White Beach. Additionally they engaged Nippon Salvage, a Japanese partner, to provide additional personnel and local equipment which eventually included a salvage tug (Hayashio Maru) and the salvage barge (Mishima).

On 24 January, SMIT/Nippon team departed the Port of Nakagusuka on board Nippon launch Miki for the first inspection of KOCAK. They assessed the hull from the surface and then boarded KOCAK and met with KOCAK's Master and Chief Engineer. The team conducted an inspection of the vessel including Cargo Holds 3A, 4, 4A (using SCBA's) and reported findings to SUPSALV and on-site MSC leadership.

2-3.3. Phoenix

Phoenix International holds the Underwater Operations contract with SUPSALV and are available for tasking via Delivery Order. A verbal delivery order was issued on 27 January to provide underwater hull inspection and repairs to USNS SGT. MATEJ KOCAK (T-AK 3005) located in Okinawa, Japan. The Verbal indicated that immediate mobilization of personnel and equipment is required in order to meet critical

Fleet operational commitments. Phoenix was tasked to mobilize equipment and needed personnel to provide underwater hull inspection and repairs. The services were to repair damage, to make USNS SGT. MATEJ KOCAK (T-AK 3005) seaworthy, and to conduct a survey of the grounding location as directed by the NAVSEA SUPSALV Representative. The first of the Phoenix team and equipment arrived at White Beach the evening the ship floated free and were ready to begin planning repairs on 4 February.

3. Salvage Operations

SUPSALV conducted the salvage of USNS KOCAK over a 13 day period. The operation could be divided into 5 phases: Damage Assessment; Flooding Containment and Restoration of Water Tightness; Development of a Salvage Plan; Fuel Offload; and Deballasting and Refloating. During that period SUPSALV, and their salvage contractor, SMIT, coordinated with KOCAK's Ship's Force and Keystone; MSC; Japanese Coast Guard; and others to execute the response. Details of each of these phases are provided in the following sections.

3-1. Initial Damage Assessment

This section describes the conditions on USNS KOCAK after SMIT's team boarded the vessel on 24 January and conditions as first observed by SUPSALV when they boarded on 25 January.

On 24 January, SMIT's Salvage Master, Jan Willem, and the Nippon Salvage Master were able to evaluate conditions on the ship and on the 25th they provided a thorough report to SUPSALV and MSC. This report included the following observations:

- The heading, list and position of the ship remained constant.
- Pollution had not been sighted since the incident took place.
- Army divers conducted a dive inspection of the starboard side (25 January) from bow to forward of accommodation. Result of observed video inspection and verbal reports indicated that there was a longitudinal crack on the starboard side in way of ballast tanks which is there several inches wide in way of outer DB/wing 4S. The crack ran through the ballast tanks and exact length could not be determined. Additionally the outer DB/wing 4P was breached.
- The bow was floating up to about frame 40. Based on soundings taken by the vessel, the stern is was clear from frame 66 to the transom.
- Propeller and rudder were clear of the reef.
- Hold 3A could only be accessed using breathing apparatus due to high CO content and fuel fumes. The hold was filled with water and on starboard side the height of the water was close to 1 meter. Due to the ship's list the water level was higher on the portside. A thin layer of fuel was visible on the water's surface. The source of the fuel was unknown and could have come from the vehicles or from a bunker tank 3P/S inner.
- The door between Hold 3A and Hold 4 was dislocated upwards for about 10 cm causing water to enter hold 4 from Hold 3A. Careful estimation was 20-30 gallons/minute.
- The crew managed to wedge the gap under the door with wooden wedges and basically stopped the water flowing into Hold 4.
- In Hold 4 on portside in way of fr 52-53 the deck was buckled. In the corner between deck and side there is a crack of about 2-3 meters (difficult to see) and some water was seeping through on deck.
- The door between Hold 4 and 4A was dislocated and slightly buckled causing seepage of water coming from Hold 4 to Hold 4A. Due to working of the vessel there was some sound.
- In Hold 4A on starboard fr 56-57, at the bottom end of the stairs on the tank top some slight buckling was visible in the deck.
- The tugs were continuing to pull the stern of the vessel to port.

- Preliminary calculations indicated the vessel was hard aground with several thousand tons of ground reaction.
- Observed draft on 24 January at high water. Readings were approximate due to incoming sea/swell:

Table 3-1. Draft Readings from 24 January observations.

	Port	STBD
Forward	18'06"	18"06"
Midships	25'06"	21'06"
Aft	Not Measured	28'03"

On 26 January, after SUPSALV's team had conducted a detailed evaluation of the vessel, the damage assessment was refined and provided to the MSC/NAVSEA/COM7THFLT team. That assessment follows:

"KOCAK is hard aground throughout the tide cycle. A dive survey has been performed to identify ground contact location. KOCAK is aground on an approximately 20-ft long coral shelf running diagonally beneath Cargo Holds 4 and 3A (see Figure 3-1). Additionally, a smaller coral pinnacle is beneath the starboard side forward of the house. Ground reactions calculations estimate KOCAK aground by approximately 3000 LT at high tide 26 February (5.7-ft above MLLW) and 10,000 LT at low tide (1.5-ft above MLLW). List is always to port and varies from approximately 1.5 degrees at high tide to 2 degrees at low tide. Vessel movement is minimal throughout the tide cycle."

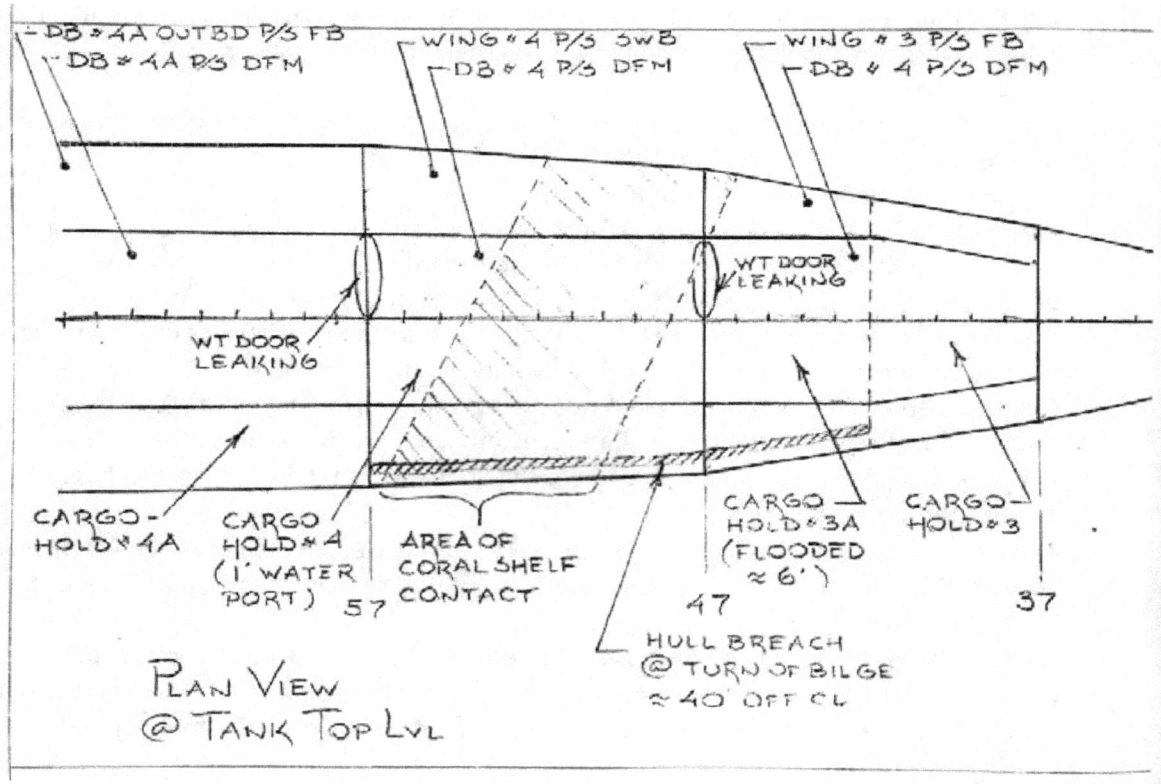

Figure 3-1: Damage and Grounding Location based on initial dive survey and early damage investigation.

"External damage identified consists solely of a longitudinal breach of the hull plating running from the forward of Frame 57 to aft of Frame 42. Hull damage runs below the bilge keel and penetrates ballast tanks 4S Outboard and 3S Outboard (see Figure 3-2). No fuel tanks have been breached."

Figure 3-2. External hull damage to the starboard side. From video taken during initial Army Special Forces dive survey.

"Internal damage consists of seawater flooding into Cargo Hold 3A. On 23 January the floodwater reached and ignited an unsecured battery in one of the cargo vehicles. The fire was extinguished and the hold secured. Over the next three days the floodwater in Cargo Hold 3A rose to approximately 6-ft which is below the waterline and indicates a slow leak rather than complete free communication. The lower deck watertight vehicle doors on the port side between Cargo Holds 3A and 4 and Cargo Holds 4 and 4A have been forced out of alignment and are no longer tight. The gaps have been plugged and communication from the flooded Cargo Hold 3A has been reduced to a manageable level. Additionally, there are minor deflections in the deck and bulkhead between Cargo Holds 4 and 4A both port and starboard."

Figure 3-3. A view from Hold 4 looking aft at the water tight door.

"CONCLUSIONS

Structural damage, while not insignificant, is not considered to be a driving factor in refloating the KOCAK. The reduction in section modulus from the damaged hull plating is less than 5%. Along the length of damage the modified section modulus is still 97% or greater than that required for normal operations. Efforts will be made to limit stresses on the hull but she is partially protected by the reef and once afloat it is only 6 miles to port. The primary objective of the salvage operations will be to reduce ground reaction to a level where KOCAK will be in position to be refloated at high tide."

It should be noted that at that time the port side bottom was inaccessible due to KOCAK's location on the reef and a detailed damage assessment in that area was not performed.

3-2. Flooding Containment and Restoration of Water Tightness

During the week of 25 February, the salvors continued to conduct inspections of damage both externally by divers and internally. No new internal damage was noted and previously identified damage remained the same. Divers inspected the starboard side in greater detail and were able to access the port side. No new breaches to the shell plating were discovered. With the dive inspection complete, the salvage team had a much better idea of where the ship was grounded. After the external and internal inspections, the salvage team felt confident that the ship was not in jeopardy of having a catastrophic structural problem, as long as conditions remained the same.

The salvage team continued to refine the POSSE computer model of the ship's condition. They believed that they would be able to refloat the vessel by only removing fluids, specifically bunkers and ballast water. That solution would be ideal since that would be the quickest and most effective means. If the team was required to remove topside weight, by craning off cargo, the process would take much longer.

On 25 January, they began offloading oily waste tanks to a waste oil containment barge that was assigned to White Beach. The ship's oily waste tanks were full from ship's force pumping contaminated flooding water into them. The offloading did not result in significant weight reduction but it did free up tank space on KOCAK for more contaminated water.

Before beginning to offload bunker fuel and ballast water, the crew needed to test and prove out the integrity of those 2 piping systems forward of the transverse bulkhead between holds 4 and 3A. Testing was scheduled for 26 January. Unfortunately weather and tides were not in the salvor's favor that week. Inclement weather was due in starting the 26th and they would continue to lose tide height throughout the week. It was recognized that bunker offloading could not be planned until the higher high tides of 2-5 February.

Figure 3-4. KOCAK grounded with U.S. Navy Commander Fleet Activities Okinawa (CFAO) White Beach waste oil containment barge, Kanto 18, alongside for collection of oily bilge water.

The salvage team discussed the idea of booming the ship with the environmental oil response representative that reported to White Beach Naval Base on 26 January. All agreed that the sea state would be problematic and that it would create a lot of useless work and added expense. Additionally, the MARENTAS representative pointed out that the boom anchors needed to hold the containment boom in place would damage the reef further.

With the ship sufficiently aground and stable on the reef, the team agreed that three tugs were not needed to hold KOCAK in position. The Master released the third tug and asked the remaining tugs to release the strain on their lines. It was believed the aft tug was causing some mild ship vibrations as it was rolling in the swells during high tide.

On 26 January, the weather front forecasted to come through held off throughout the day which allowed continued pumping of slop waste oil and contaminated flooding water to the waste oil containment barge. Ship's force was also able to successfully test and prove out the integrity of the fuel oil transfer lines. Upon learning of this, the ship began transferring fuel from tanks adjacent to grounding damage to empty fuel tanks away from the inner bottom. This reduced the potential for oil spillage if the shell plating and inner bottom plates failed.

Captain Edberg, MSC Yokohama, was able to secure a DLA fuel tanker, (SLNC PAX out of Annapolis, MD) for bunker off-loading. ETA of the tanker was 1 Feb. POSSE computer modeling at that time showed that at high tide the day before, 25 January, the ship was approximately 2800 LT aground but closer to 10,000 LT at low tide. The team anticipated the requirement to offload ballast water but at that time they had not discussed it with the Japanese Coast Guard so they were unclear on the legality of doing it.

CAPT Baumann recommended, and MSC agreed, that SUPSALV should bring in our underwater welding contractor to conduct critical repairs to the hull prior to moving the ship to the drydock for permanent repairs. SUPSALV initiated the tasking and asked the SUPSALV underwater ship husbandry team to coordinate their arrival with the ship floating free.

Lastly, the team discussed the idea of using the time between now and when the fuel ship arrives to begin offloading topside cargo. The amount of weight removed would be limited but because it was all located on deck, it would lower the center of gravity and improve the deballasted ship's stability. MSC initiated that request with port ops, and U.S. Army who had Landing craft at White Beach.

On 27 January the salvors took a step back in progress against the flooding on the ship. Specifically, the patching in Hold 3A, which had been holding up since right after the grounding, gave way over night on the January 26. The result was that water levels rose in 3A and the head pressure exceeded the capability of the temporary patching under the dislodged watertight doors between Holds 3A and 4 and under the door between Holds 4 and 4A. Water levels in all three holds began to rise again. Ship's force and the SMIT/Nippon salvors were initially able to keep up and were making head way against the flooding waters but due to some hose ruptures they lost pumping capacity and water levels began to rise again. At that point, SUPSALV indicated more help was needed and MSC contacted CTF-76 with an immediate request for assistance. USS BONHOMME RICHARD (LHD 6) which was steaming in the region answered the call and within 15 minutes the team received a response saying they were mobilizing. The Damage Control Chief Petty Officer was aboard within 2 hours making assessments and a Rescue and Assistance team was rigging equipment into the spaces within 4 hours. By 2200 that evening, reports from the ship indicated the water levels were retreating in all 3 holds.

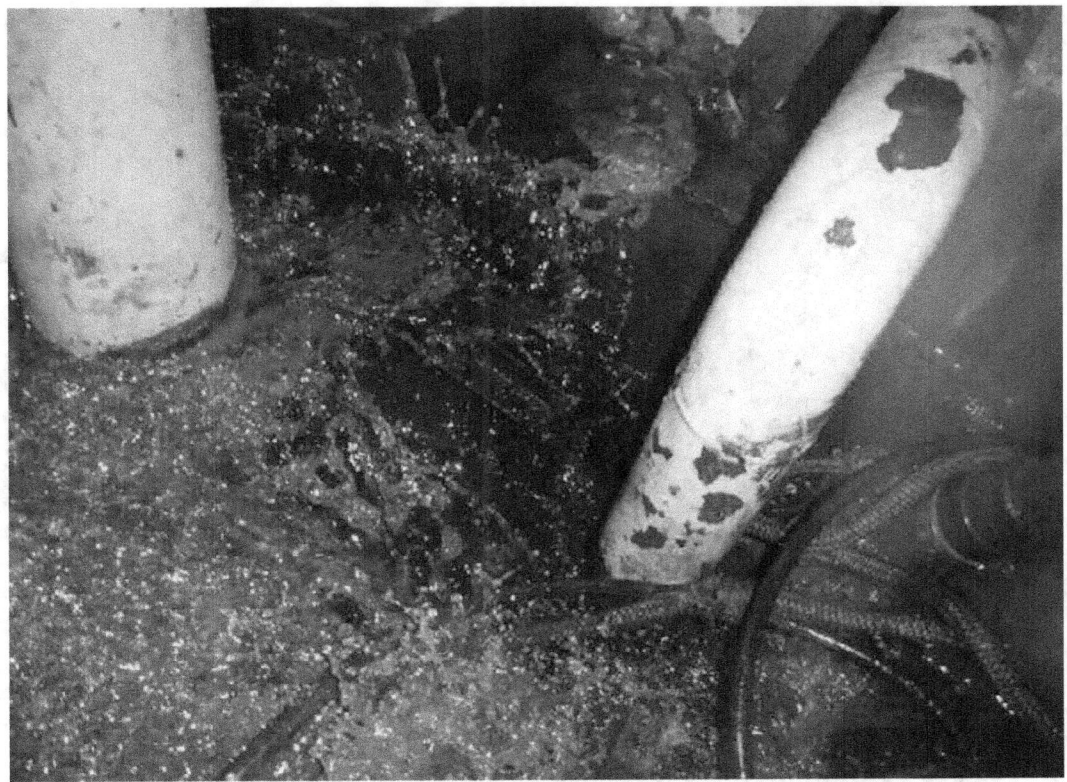

Figure 3-5. Seawater freely flowing from sump in Hold 3A.

The USS BONHOMME RICHARD sailors integrated with the salvage crew for the next couple of days and SUPSALV authorized increasing the number of commercial salvors on site to give the KOCAK engineers some much needed rest. The number of commercial salvors authorized increased by ten Nippon Salvage personnel and seven SMIT salvage personnel bringing the total assigned to 21. All were to arrive on station by early evening of 28 January. Nippon Salvage was also tasked to provide their salvage barge, Mishima, to support the team with berthing facilities, slops storage, and crane services as needed.

The recharged and reinforced salvors continued pumping down the 3 Holds. Once the water level in Hold 3A was down far enough, they worked plugging the cargo door, this time from Hold 3A side. As they continued to get the water level down, it was easier to get to the crux of the problem and begin plugging the leaks. The sailors and salvors achieved success with the cargo door between Holds 3A and 4. They re-established the water tight boundary by reseating door and dogging it tight.

Over the next several days KOCAK continued to remain stable and showed no signs of serious structural failure. Despite the arrival of strong winds and heavy seas, the salvage team made excellent progress in controlling the flooding in Holds 3A / 4 / 4A. The game changer was the arrival of the USS BONHOMME RICHARD Damage Control teams and the follow-on arrival of the additional SMIT and Nippon salvage mechanics. Figure 3-6 shows a team of BONHOMME RICHARD sailors knee deep in Cargo Hold 3A.

Figure 3-6. USS BONHOMME RICHARD Damage Control Team members conducting dewatering operations.

Figure 3-7. Pump rigged in sump of Cargo Hold 3A. Evidence of oily residue on bulkhead bears witness to higher water levels.

With the water levels lowered in all three previously flooded holds, the crew were better able to assess the damage. The salvors found 3 significant leaks in Hold 3A. Two areas had cracked welds between the tank top and vertical beams, and the third was a hole where a person could stick their hand through in the deck. A more detailed depiction of the internal damages is provided in Figure 3-10 and images of damage and actions to stabilize the damage are provided in the next few pages.

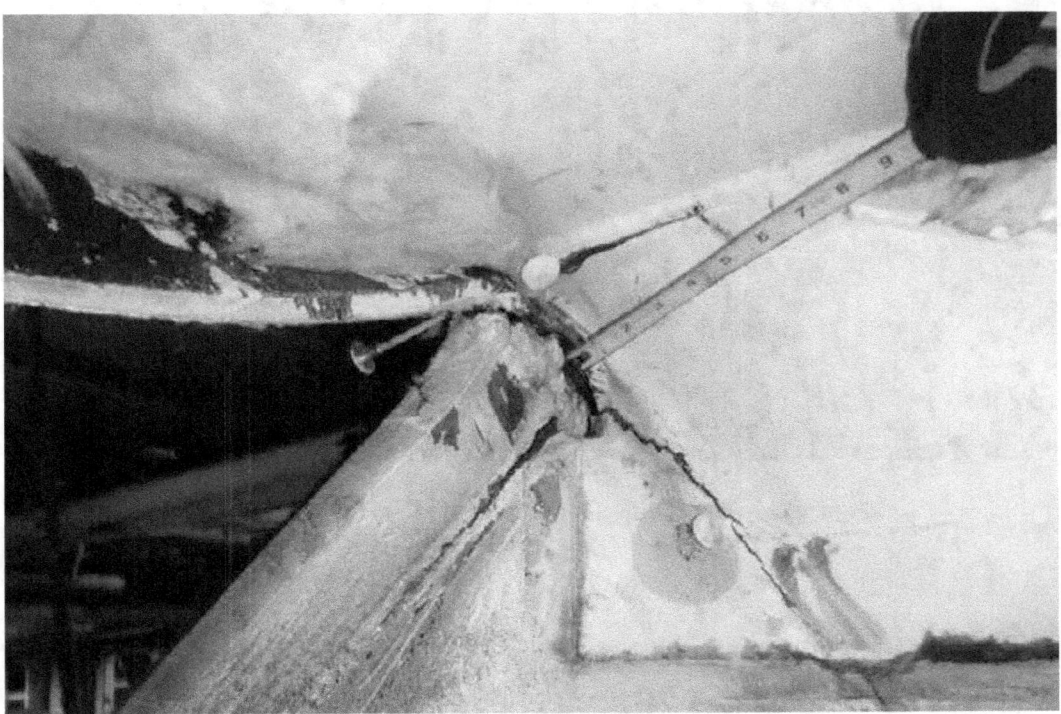

Figure 3-8. Bulkhead Stiffener Cracks in Hold 3A.

Figure 3-9. SMIT salvors assessing leak rates in Hold 3A.

Figure 3-10. Hold 4 port side tank top buckling resulted in stress on this ladder.

An additional key to pumping the spaces dry was the availability of the slops barge. Having a place to pump oily waste was critical to keeping the levels low and not discharging any oil into the sea. When sea levels were running high, it was unsafe to keep that barge alongside USNS KOCAK. Also, it had to be offloaded when the tanks reached capacity. During those periods, KOCAK pumped to its own waste oil tanks.

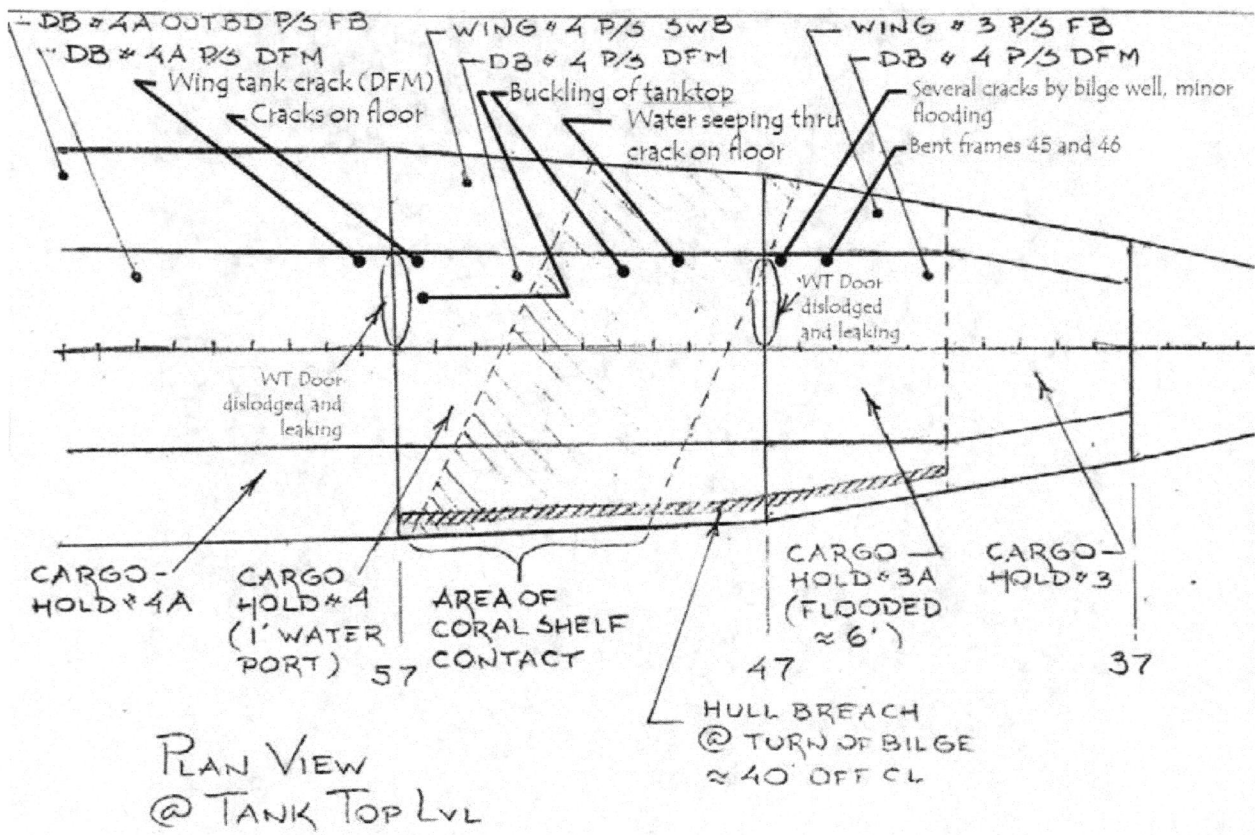

Figure 3-11. Internal damage following detailed survey.

A second new discovery was that the port permanent ballast tank on the outboard side of Hold 3A was open to the sea. This ballast tank had been filled with an iron ore slurry later identified as Magnetite & Hematite. A review of the MSDS indicated that there were no acute symptoms for incidental contact and very limited concern for environmental issues.

On the days leading up to the higher tide cycles, the team continued to work on stopping / slowing the ingress of water into holds 3A, 4 and 4A. The team made excellent progress in slowing the leakage in 3A at the port side, aft bulkhead. The leaks in that area were at the welds on the I-beams on the aft bulkhead at the intersection with the deck. They're very difficult to access and plug. But the team slowed the flooding to the point that they were not concerned about how much water the ship would take on after having to shut down pumping operations during float off.

Figure 3-12. Patched and cleaned Hold 3A sump awaiting float off.

On 29 January, Nippon Salvage conducted another dive survey of the hull. After reviewing the video which provided better detail than the first preliminary dive survey video, the team had a much better understanding of how tight it would be to remove the ship from its grounded position. Specifically, the clearance between the prop/rudder and the reef was approximately 1 meter. During the lightering evolution, the ship was expected to trim down by the stern. The reason for that is simple. The weight was being removed from forward and amidships tanks and the stern would predictably drop as a result. It was planned that to better monitor what was happening during the lightering and deballasting evolution, Nippon Salvage divers would be staged to go in the water to periodically give a real time assessment of where the ship's propeller and rudders were relative to the reef.

Figure 3-13. Propeller clearance to reef from 29 January dive survey video.

3-3. Development of a Salvage Plan

After the damage assessment was complete and assessing the ship as stable, the Salvage team developed the beginnings of a plan for removing USNS KOCAK from the reef. The plan could be divided into three phases.

- Removal of water from flooded holds and control/limit ingress of water.
- Offload fuel oil to lighten the ship and reduce exposure to major leaks by removing fuel adjacent to double bottom.
- Deballast seawater from ballast tanks to further lighten ship.   This effort would be timed to coincide with higher high tide to support float off.

By 31 January, SUPSALV and the SMIT/Nippon salvors had been with the ship for a week. During that week they had determined that the ship could float off if the tide was high enough and the liquid load was reduced enough but the details of the requirements were still being refined.

Two diving surveys had been conducted, the initial, by U.S. Army Special Forces divers on 25 January and a more detailed survey by Nippon salvage divers on 30 January. These confirmed the limited external damages to the ship's hull. SUPSALV's Naval Architect, Vince Jarecki and MSC's Naval Architect, Paul Handler worked together to model the ship in its current condition and assessed that the structural damage, while not insignificant, would not hamper the refloating of the ship.   The refloating plan incorporated the fact that Holds 3A, 4 and 4A, which had previously been partially flooded, were currently dewatered and would remain empty during the refloating process. Figure 3-14 is the POSSE profile and plan view defining the liquid and cargo loads on the ship prior to beginning the refloating process.

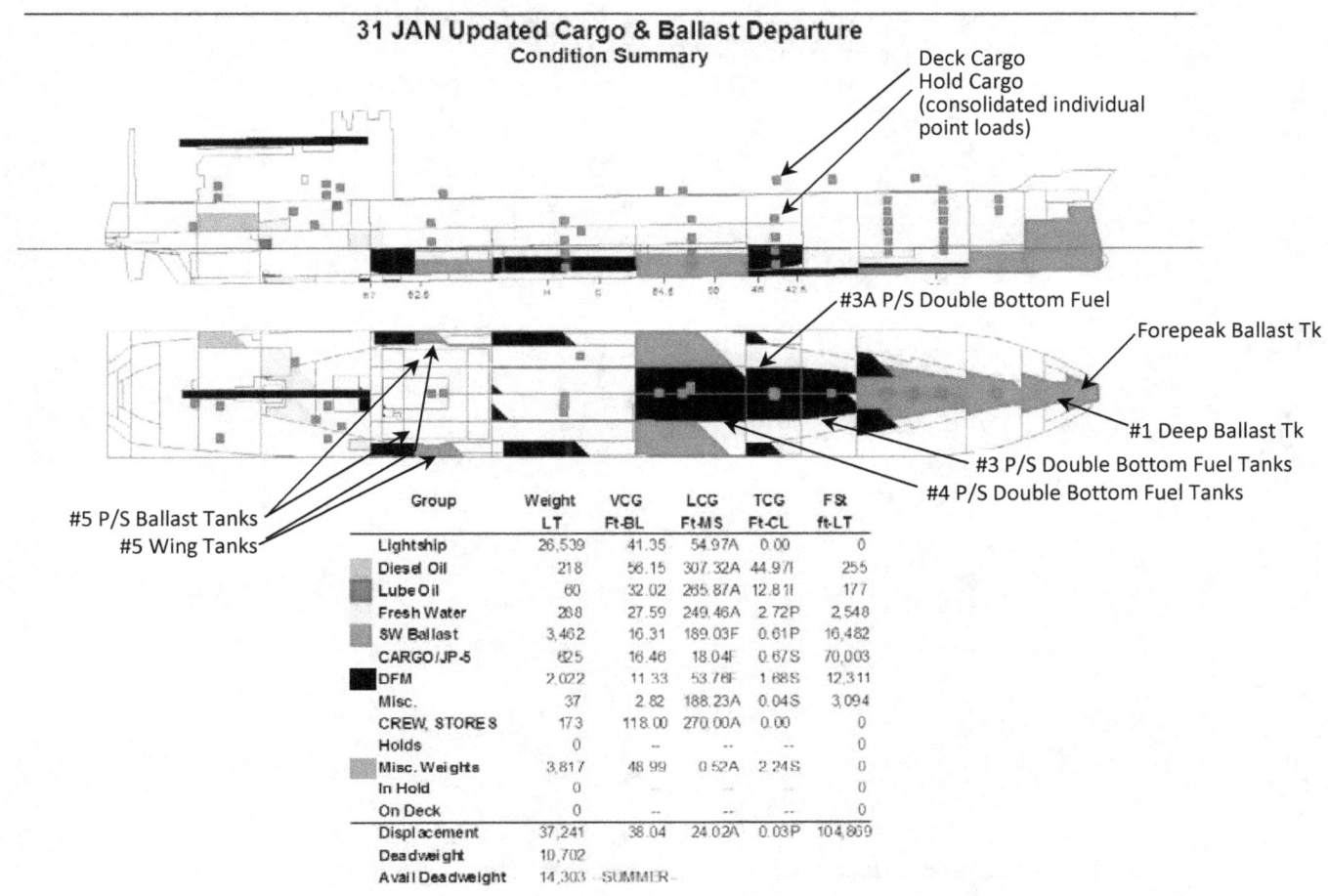

Figure 3-14. POSSE Profile and Plan View of Liquid Loads and Deck and Hold Cargo.

With ground reactions calculations estimating KOCAK aground by approximately 3000 LT at high tide 26 February (5.7-ft above MLLW) and 10,000 LT at low tide (1.5-ft above MLLW) both fuel oil and ballast water would need to be removed from the ship to reduce ground reaction to a level where KOCAK will be in position to be float at high tide.

MSC had tasked a small tanker, SLNC PAX, to receive fuel from KOCAK. The team planned to offload approximately 10,000 gallons of diesel from Wing Tanks #3 P/S, Inboard Double Bottom Tanks #4 P/S, and Inboard Double Bottom Tanks #4A P/S. It was estimated the fuel transfer could be accomplished in approximately 10 hours.

The following day, 3 February, it was planned that enough ballast water would be removed from the ship to raise the bow off the coral shelf and allow her to float free at high tide. Selected ballast tanks included Wing Tank 4 Port and Stbd, Ballast Tanks 5 port and stbd, the forepeak tank, and wing tanks 5 port and stbd. It was anticipated that the ship would float off 30 minutes before high tide on 3 February. (6 pm local time). By Friday 30 January, the team had made enough progress that they felt confident they could hold the water levels down in the holed spaces that the initial Liquid Offload Plan was briefed to the Japanese Coast Guard at the 1800 meeting. This brief was refined on 1 February, finalizing the fuel tanks to be pumped, the timeline for lightering fuel and the timeline for debalasting. That plan is included as Attachment A, Liquid Offload Plan.

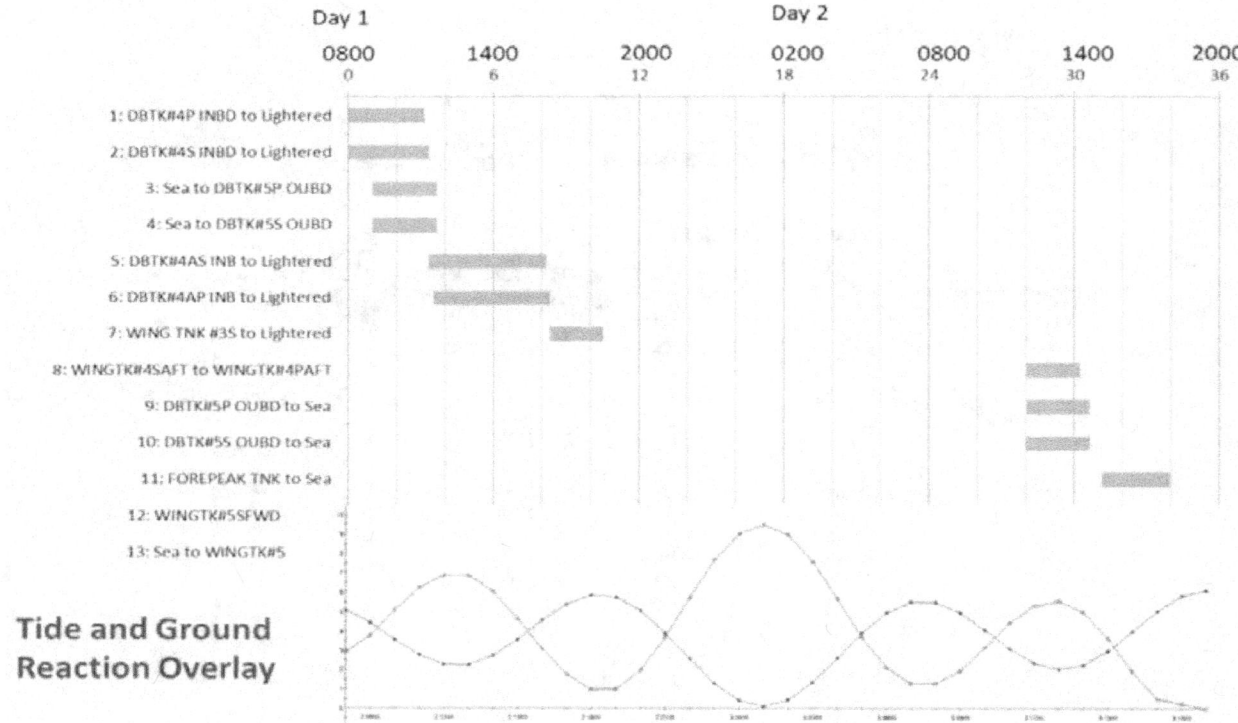

Figure 3-15. Liquid offload timeline as briefed on 1 February to the Japanese Coast Guard.

The tide cycle would support float off attempts on 3, 4 and 5 February. If the team was not successful by that point, considerations would have to be made for cargo offload to gain additional buoyancy and to allow refloating at lower tides.

3-4. Petroleum Offload

On Monday, 2 February 2015 the salvage team began the fuel offload of USNS KOCAK. The Liquid Offload plan dated 1 February (Attachment A) detailed the diesel oil tanks to be lightered. MSC had retasked a long term lease tanker, SLNC PAX, to steam to White Beach. SLNC PAX arrived in Nakagusuku Bay at 0600 on Sunday 1 February and docked at the Army Pier at White Beach at that morning.

The plan was to breast the tanker, SLNC PAX off MSC's KOCAK using Nippon's salvage barge, Mishima, which had a beam of 24 meters. The Nippon barge depth was 4 meters and draft approximately 2 meters. SLNC PAX design draft is 7 meters. The most recent survey of the bottom adjacent to KOCAK showed bottom depths between 6 and 8 meters on the port side just forward of amidships. Since the shallow water would prevent SLNC PAX from going directly alongside the Nippon barge was employed. Figure 3-16 shows the planned arrangement of the vessels during the fuel offload.

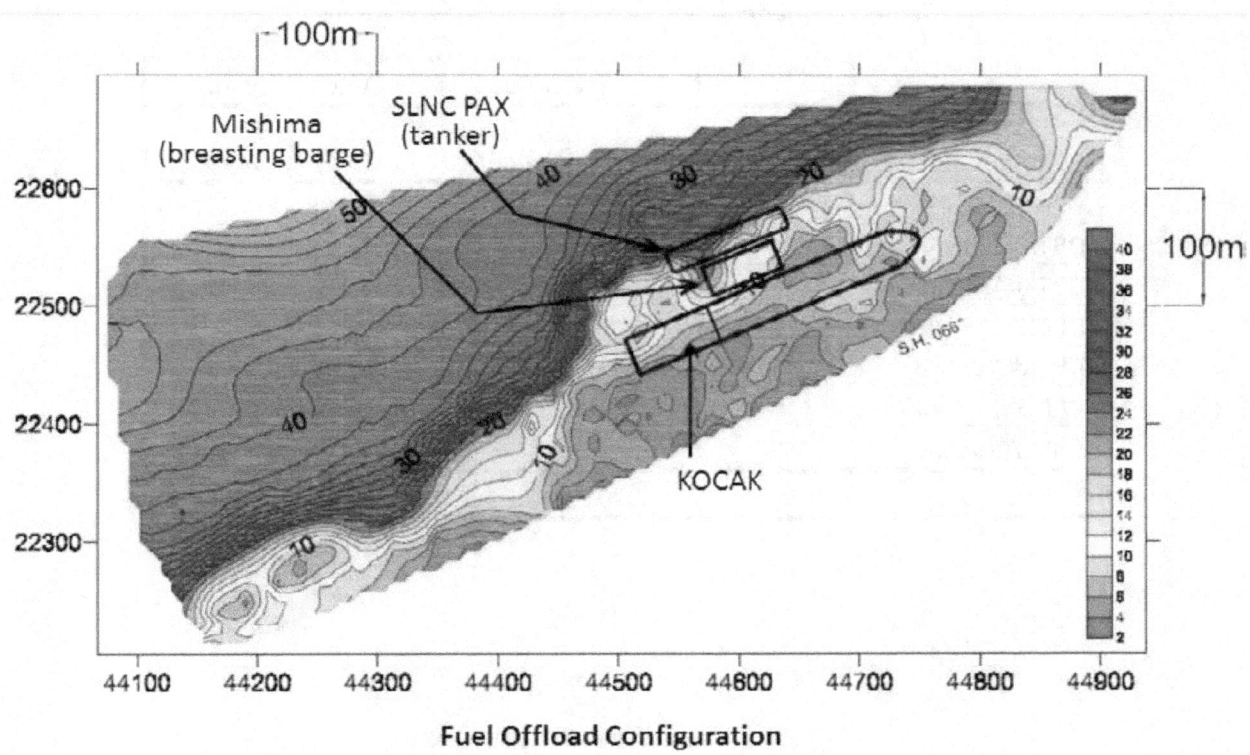

Fuel Offload Configuration

Figure 3-16. Arrangement of KOCAK, Mishima, and SLNC PAX during defueling operations.

The tanker departed White Beach pier at 0615 Monday and moored against Mishima at 0830. Mishima had been placed along KOCAK's port side at 1400 on 1 February. She had been loaded with fuel hoses and fenders to support the operation. Hoses were run without delay and DFM pumping began at 0942. The salvage team reported the pumping at a rate greater than 1000 bbl per hour.

As reported during the 1800 briefings, the Japanese Coast Guard's highest priority was to avoid oil spillage. The offload plan was crafted to begin pumping as early as possible in the morning and to be finished before dark. The favorable weather conditions and better than planned offload rate provided the opportunity to offload more fuel than originally planned. Table 3-2 shows the planned and actual fuel offloaded on 2 February.

On 2 February, the Progress Meeting with the Coast Guard, again held at 1800, MSC leadership reported the pumping was nearly complete. The planned tankage was pumped down by 1615 but the Naval Architects calculated the weight of the ship based on draft readings and tank levels and indicated that the removal of an additional 300 tons would be advantageous and feasible with the remaining time until sunset. This fuel was taken from 4 port and stbd wing tanks. Figure 3-17 shows a port side view of the SLNC PAX (on left), Mishima, and KOCAK during the fuel offload process.

Table 3-2. Planned and Actual fuel offload volumes.

Comp	Mat'l	Planned Offload		Actual Offload	
		Vol (bbl)	Vol (gal)	Vol (bbl)	Vol (gal)
WING TNK #3S	F76	1112	46704	1,188	49896
DBTK#4P INBD	F76	1573	66066	1,528	64176
DBTK#4S INBD	F76	1662	69804	1,523	63966
DBTK#4AP INB	MGO	2427	101934	2,377	99834
DBTK#4AS INB	MGO	2427	101934	2,332	97944
WINGTK#4PAFT	MGO	0	0	636	26712
WINGTK#4SAFT	MGO	0	0	1,503	63126
TOTAL		9201	386442	11087	465654

Figure 3-17. Tanker, SLNC PAX, Nippon salvage barge, Mishima, and USNS KOCAK during the 2 February fuel offload. As portrayed, calm seas supported the defueling operation.

Throughout the fuel offload process, sea water was added to the ballast tanks to keep KOCAK firmly on the bottom during the high tides. At the end of the day, 11,000 barrels of fuel were offloaded to the SLNC PAX. No oil leaks occurred.

3-5. De-ballasting and Float Off

Weather again cooperated with the salvage team for the 3 February deballasting evolution. The monthly tide cycle was returning to the higher high tides for 3 days beginning 3 February. This was the reason for the timing of the defueling/deballasting effort. A Go / No-go decision was made at 0800. The following observations / events took place during the deballasting operation:

- A work boat from Mishima positioned buoys on reef marking pinnacles to be avoided by the tugs and when KOCAK should float free.
- Nippon Salvage placed divers on standby in case the team needed to observe the clearance between the propellers and the reef.
- A new crack leaking water near frame 57 on edge of tank top was reported (from the ship's hull working on reef).
- Deballasting commenced at 0900.
- Small sheen spotted by KOCAK crewman. Pumping stopped during investigation. The Master and Chief (Engineer) suspect that this "burp" found its way into the ballast pump line from a previous operation. It likely burped during the initial deballasting the forepeak or #5 wing tanks. KOCAK and SMIT engineering team closed and isolated the ballast pump and pulled strainer. No issues were found and it was ruled an anomaly how small amount of oil became entrained. Deballasting re-started after the investigation at approximately 1000 hours.
- Suction from Double bottom tanks No. 5 (P/S) proved to be unsuccessful. Ship's crew informed the salvors that the tanks were rarely pumped down and the suction lines appeared to become air bound when suction was applied. These tanks represented a major midships source of the ballasting water removal plan and alternative weight reduction options would need to be identified before the high tide.
- The salvors removed additional water from the Forepeak and # 1 Deep ballast tanks to make up for the loss of buoyancy from not pumping No. 5 (P/S). Compressed air was applied to # 4 Wing ballast tanks P/S.
- Loss of midships weight reduction and increase in bow weight reduction raised concerns that propeller/running gear could impact reef where clearance was only 1 meter in grounded condition.
- At approximately 1700 the combination of the rising tide and deballasting forward had resulted in noticeable movement of the bow as it floated free of the forward coral shelf.
- Shifted focus of pumping to offloading the Wing Tank #5Fwd Stbd to heel the ship off the starboard pinnacle.
- At 1700, KOCAK Ships force commenced rocking the Morgan Crain starboard to port in an attempt to break the ship free.
- At 1700, two tugs with a combined bollard pull of 100 MT began to periodically take strain on the stern. Figures 3-18 and 3-19 provide a graphic and photographic documentation of the extraction arrangement.
- At 1730 KOCAK floated free of the reef without damage to propeller or rudder.
- Corrected list (2 degrees port) and KOCAK was spun around (by tugs) and steamed back to White Beach on her own power.

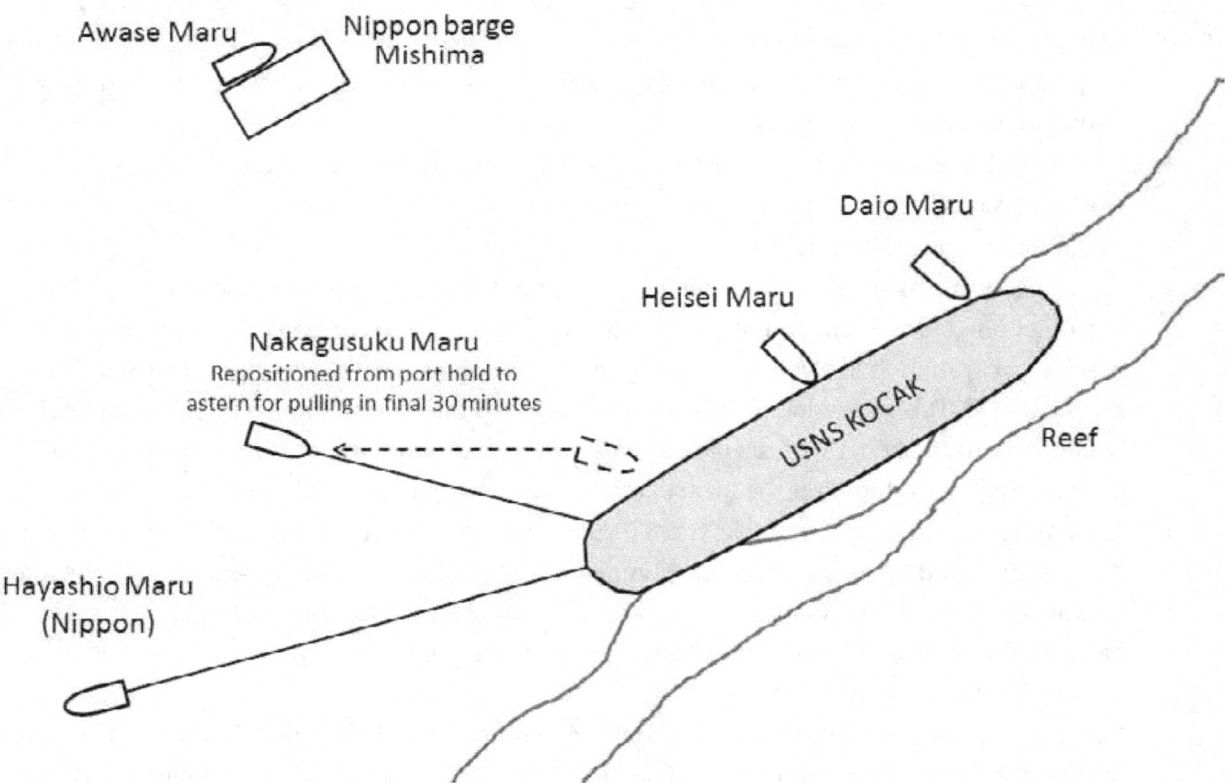

Figure 3-18. Arrangement of tugs to support float off of KOCAK on 3 February.

Figure 3-19. Two tugs pulling KOCAK (astern) and two tugs stabilizing KOCAK's bow at approximately 1700 on 3 February.

Additional information concerning the salvage planning, fuel offload, and deballasting actions can be found by reading Attachment D, POSSE Report. The report also documents some of the observations and recommendations concerning the POSSE program made by SUPSALV's Naval Architect during the operation.

4. Post Salvage Actions

After KOCAK was successfully pulled from the reef without contact of propeller or rudder she was trimmed to an even keel, steamed back to White Beach on her own power and was assisted to the pier bow out. At 1942 the first line was heaved over to the pier. Docking complete, accommodation ladder deployed, it was the end of long couple of days and a major accomplishment. Port Operations had laid oil containment boom under the pier and by 2115 the boom was pulled around the ship providing a measure of protection against possible oil spill.

Figure 4-1. KOCAK back at the pier the evening of 3 February.

That same evening an advance party consisting of a SUPSALV Underwater Ships Husbandry engineer, Jacob Nessel, and a team lead from Phoenix International, SUPSALV's diving support contractor, arrived in preparation for making temporary repairs to USNS KOCAK. The remainder of the Phoenix crew of underwater welders arrived on 5 February.

Nippon Divers performed a post salvage video survey the morning of 4 February provided SUPSALV, MSC and Phoenix repair specialists with the first clear picture of the damage to the hull after it slid off the reef. In particular, the salvors wanted to see the extent of the damage to the hull in the area where coral prevented detailed evaluation when the ship was aground. This survey would serve as a starting point for developing the plans for conducting temporary repairs.

Because of the damage USNS KOCAK received during its grounding a U.S. Coast Guard (USCG) 835 was issued directing "No Sail" to KOCAK until USCG and American Bureau of Shipping (ABS), the classification society for KOCAK, approve temporary repairs made in White Beach.   To support evaluation of the repairs, ABS sent a representative to provide oversight of the temporary repairs.

4-1. Temporary Repairs to Allow Sailing to Repair Facility

4-1.1. Repair Overview.

USCG and ABS representatives arrived on site on 4 February. After the Nippon dive survey, a walk through and conversations with ship operator, Keystone as well as SUPSALV repair team including Phoenix lead, and Clint Lawler, Navy Repair Officer was conducted. They agreed to a tentative plan that would confirm/assure strength of the ships structure, reestablish water tight integrity, and shore up dewatering capacity during the transit. The tentative plan addressed repairs to shell plating and repairs inside the ship. The full plan is provided as Attachment E at the end of this report.

4-1.2. Repairs to Shell Plating

Restore Port Shell Plating: Weld Repairs (P1, P2, P3)

- Arrest/remove cracks (arc gouging, drill stop (min dia = 2X crack width), VT, MT).
- Port shell plate sealing (P1, P2, P3) with doubler plates (3 locations) or elliptical head patches as required to fit (min ¼" plate for doublers, 3/8" plate for elliptical heads).
- Underwater wet welding IAW ABS approved procedures.

Figure 4-2 provides an overview of the shell planning damage and repair locations.

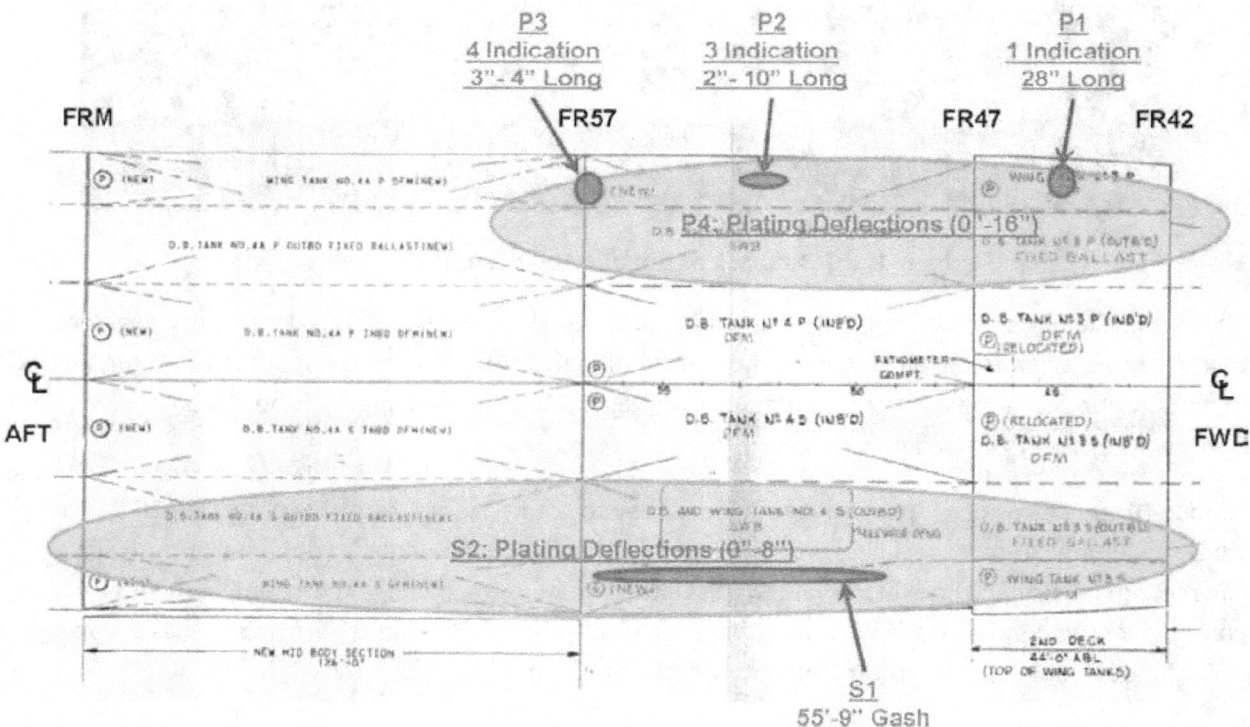

Figure 4-2. Shell damage and repair planning.

4-1.3. Repairs inside the Double Bottom, tanks, and Cargo Holds

Inside the ship, the repairs would take place between the double bottom and the tank tops. An overview of those plans can be seen in Figure 4-3. Those planned repairs included:

Isolate Port tanks 3A, 4 and 4A from the Cargo Holds: P8, P9, P10 and P11

- Crack in 3A (FB) - weld repair tank top to Cargo Hold boundary.
- Crack in 4A (FO) - epoxy repair inside tank with shoring inside the tank to support.
- Cracks in 4 (SWB) - epoxy repair inside tank with shoring inside the tank to support.

Isolate 4A wing fuel tank from adjacent ballast tanks.

- Epoxy repair inside tank with shoring inside the tank to support.

Isolate 4P D/B from 4S D/B, cross flooding tubes with mechanical blanking plates: (SMIT)

- Mechanical Patches at cross connect tubes utilize 3/8" plate circular patch to cover 26" diameter tubes at upper end of each (port and stbd) tube. Circular patch is split to fit inside manhole and installed with 1-3/4" thick neoprene gasket. Gasket is compressed with turnbuckles jacking against the patch plate and the overhead of the cross connect tube box structure or strongbacks and j-Bolts. Flood water would put each patch and gasket in compression.

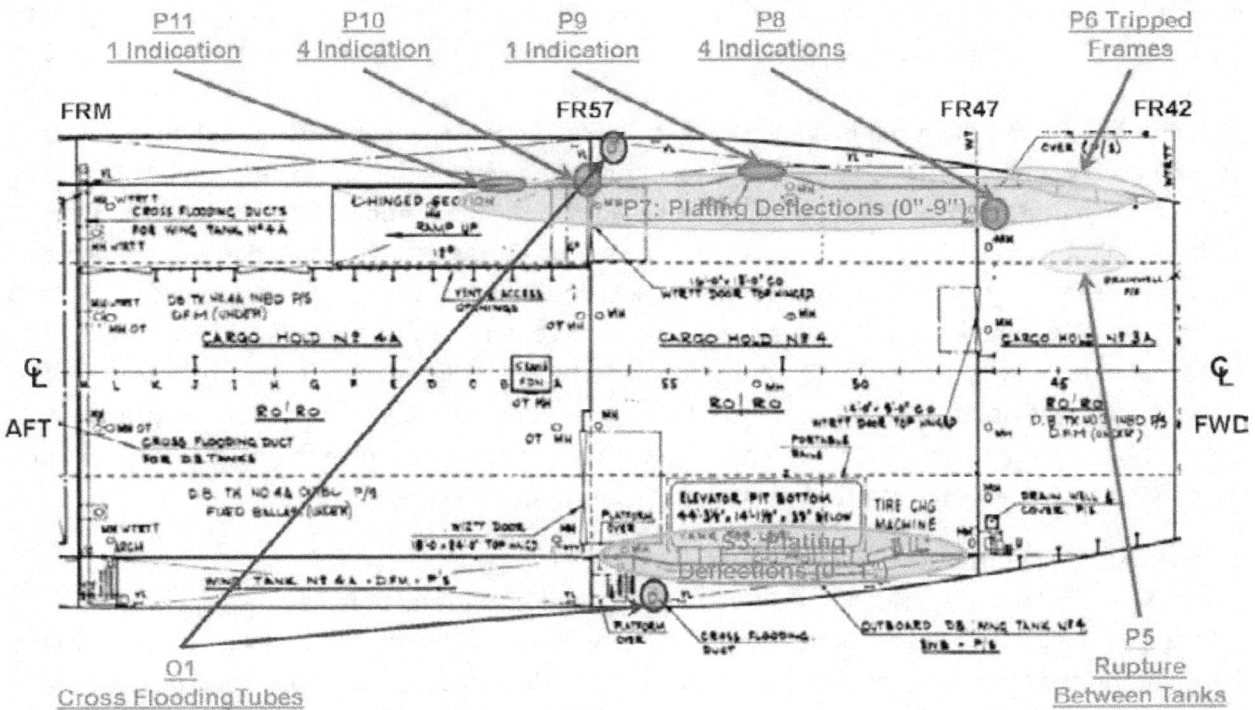

Figure 4-3. Overview of repairs within double bottom, tanks, and holds.

Restore Cargo Hold watertight integrity between holds 4 and 4A with door modification (P14).

- Cut bottom of door to match tank top contour
- Replace existing shoe plate with ½" shoe plate
- Install door seal channel below the shoe plate
- Cut back the bottom 24" of the outboard side of the door to match the contour of the bent frame and modify side seal channel to match contour
- Secure closed door with turnbuckles to replace upper and lower door locks that were removed to facilitate door opening.

4-1.4. Conduct of Repairs

With a tentative repair plan in place, SUPSALV's UWSH team began their repairs. On 7 February, the Phoenix dive team completed diving inspection of the port and starboard sides. This inspection mapped the damages relative to each plate of the ship's shell. It provided a highly detailed drawing and analysis of each indication.

One of the requirements for the repairs was to conduct analysis of the steel so the correct welding material and process was selected for each repair. Samples were collected and mailed to San Diego where a lab performed the analysis. This was deemed faster than using a Japanese analysis service due to the turn-around time the local lab required.

A second requirement was the process for identifying and arresting shell plating crack ends. To identify the actual end of the crack, a diver would use a Magnetic Particle Tester to perform Magnetic Testing (MT) of each crack to identify where the indication ended. The Magnetic Particle Testing equipment Phoenix brought with them was malfunctioning and required replacement parts to get it functioning. By 10 February, a new MT Yoke was delivered and the MT equipment was made operational. The team began MT'ing, drill stopping and arc-gouging shell plating along the starboard site which ABS had verbally indicated was not going to require the large box patch. As that determination was not finalized, the UWSH team also continued to plan for the large box patch installation. If ABS held fast to their preliminary determination and the construction of the starboard box patch could be eliminated, the team had roughly 5 days of doubler plate installs on port shell in 9 locations to complete. Phoenix International, who holds SUPSALV's Undersea Operations Contract and performed these repairs, provided a completion report that summarizes the repairs and provides some observations. An excerpt from that report is provided as Attachment G at the end of the document.

4-1.4.1 Shell Welding

SUPSALV's UWSH team focused on the bottom repairs initially. Bottom preparations began on 10 February with a detailed inspection and on 12 February, the team determined that 4 of the 9 initial port side indications were not hull breaches and were not affecting watertight integrity. That reduced the number of shell patches to five. All indications were renamed according to their location.

Results of hull material testing were received on 12 February. The lab analysis indicated that two welding process were necessary to patch the ship's hull. Three patches would require Hydroweld Electrode procedures/materials and two patches would use the Nickel Electrode procedures/materials.

Repairs to these five breaches were conducted over the period of 12 to 15 February. 225 inches of production welding was accomplished. In some cases, an elliptical patch or box patch was used in place of the planned doubler plates due to the extreme contour of the hull, the longest of which was 41" x 8". Figure 4-4 shows the templating of a dome patch on port side of the hull.

Figure 4-4. Dome patch templating on port side of USNS KOCAK. The repair team used dome patches to compensate for the distortions the hull plating.

4-1.4.2 Inner bottom and tank welding

Much of the inner bottom and tank welding depended on cleaning the space for entry and hot work. The Marine Chemist, who was hired to support the operation, arrived on 13 February and from that point on, interior welding began to move forward. Loss of tank integrity hampered production. For example, the team would clean a tank for inspection, only to find standing fuel oil in it some hours later when welding was scheduled. The team determined that the failures in some of the tanks cascaded into other tanks. Figure 4-5 shows the inner connectivity of tanks and compartments from #3A Fixed Ballast to 4A wing Fuel.

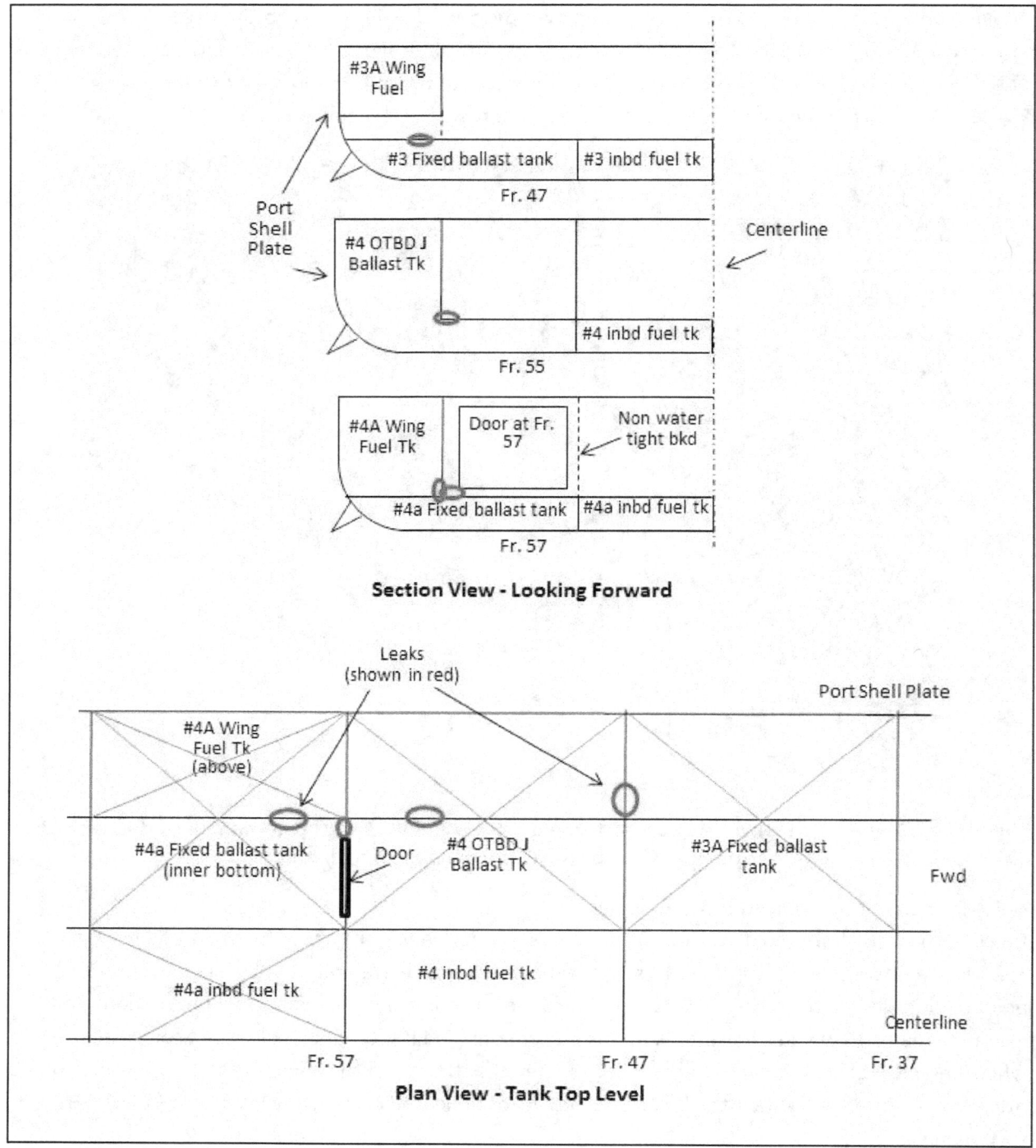

Figure 4-5. Plan and Sectional views of tank top level leaks.

The chemist concluded much of the fixed ballast tanks were saturated in DFM so the tanks were drilled and purged with carbon dioxide to inert them prior to and during welding. After welding was complete, the holes were tapped and plugs inserted. By 17 February, with underwater welding completed, there were 3 separate teams of welder/divers working inside the ship. On 19 February, tank/cargo hold integrity had been restored.

4-1.4.3   Cargo Door between Hold 4 and 4A

To ensure the ship was ready to sail, SEA 00C ordered two more welders on station on 10 February. They arrived from San Diego in the evening on 12 February with checked and carry-on luggage that included doubler plate material certified for the type repairs being accomplished. They were on the job 13 February and were assigned the job of making the bulkhead vehicle door between holds 4 and 4A watertight. The modified plan included the following:

- Cutting bottom of door to match tank top contour
- Replacing existing shoe plate with new ½" shoe plate
- Cut back bottom 24" of the outboard side of the door to match the contour of the bent frame and modify side seal channel to match contour.
- Weld new shoe plate to deck
- Securing closed door with turnbuckles to replace the upper and lower door locks that were removed to facilitate door opening.

Figure 4-6. 4-4A Watertight door repairs. Left hand corner welds were strengthening and sealing outboard bulkhead of compartment and adjacent wing fuel tank.

By 19 February, repairs to the door were completed and final welding was taking place on the bulkheads adjacent to that door. On 20 February, the final plate required to seal bulkhead 57 was installed outboard of the Cargo Door. The door was closed and sealed in place completing the above water portion of the repairs.   Figure 4-6 shows the outboard of the watertight door looking forward from hold 4A after repairs were completed. The chains were used to dog the door tight following weld repairs.

A salvage pump was rigged in hold 3A and a SMIT Damage Control team of 4 persons who were to ride the ship to its repair port was briefed and readied for getting underway. The SUPSALV/Phoenix repair team packed up their welding equipment and demobilized. On 1 March, 2015, prior to KOCAK sailing, the on-board SMIT Salvage Team, which would ride the ship to the shipyard, were transferred off the SUPSALV contract and placed under a contract arrangement between Keystone and SMIT.

5. Environmental Preparedness and Damage Assessment

When an 821 foot long, 48,000 ton ship hits a coral reef at 18 knots, you know something is going to happen. At a minimum, as the saying goes, "that will leave a mark". The worst case would be that the ship breaks up and the reef breaks up. Initial post grounding observations indicated that the ship was holding together but the concern that there could be oil released prompted the development of an Environmental Response Plan. Because the reef belongs to the Japanese Nation, and the U.S. had an obligation to acknowledge the environmental damage, a Post Salvage Ecological Assessment was performed to determine the extent of the damage. The "Plan" and the "Assessment" are addressed in the following paragraphs.

5-1.1. Environmental Response Plan

While USNS KOCAK is a government asset under U.S. Transportation Command control, the ship's operator is Keystone. To minimize loss to their ship, the U.S. Navy assumed control of the salvage operation and MSC tasked SUPSALV to conduct the operation. USNS KOCAK's Operator, Keystone Shipping Company was responsible for damages associated with the operation of the vessel. The largest liability, once safety of personnel was assured, is the environmental damage the spilling of oil could do to the near shore environment of Nakagusuku Bay.

Keystone was tasked by MSC to prepare a contingency plan to respond to any potential loss of oil. ECM Maritime Services (ECM) who is the contracted U.S. Spill Manager for Keystone was called upon to provide onsite pollution prevention and environmental expertise during the refloating operation. ECM turned to MARENTAS who is based in the Far East and has contacts in the operating area. MARENTAS representative, Natasha Lippens, arrived at White Beach on 25 January, assessed the situation on board, the environmental conditions in the bay and shoreline, and the oil spill response capabilities in the region and developed a plan for mitigation of oil spill risks.

MARENTAS contracted with Maritime Disaster Prevention Center (MDPC), which is an Oil Spill Response (OSR) organization with assets and employees on the island, to provide equipment and teams to support the operation. Ms. Lippens designed a response plan that included two skimmers being placed in the water and manned during the refloating operation. One vessel was capable of conducting free skimming operations with a 7M aluminum pole to spread its boom and the other tug boat would operate with a second support vessel spreading a 200M boom in a J configuration. Fixed boom around the grounded ship was not deemed practical due to the high sea state in the bay when weather conditions worsened and that the boom moorings would damage the reef.

Once the response plan was prepared, it was reviewed and approved by MSC and briefed to the Japanese Coast Guard on 30 January. The plan was finalized after these briefings and is available as Attachment C for more detailed study.

On 2 February, the day of the defueling, the oil response vessels and teams were placed in standby but remained in port approximately 7 to 8 NM from KOCAK. The OSR coordinator remained at White Beach in contact with the salvage crews on the ship and was prepared to initiate response if it was required.

On 3 February, during refloating operations, the tug and support vessel was deployed to the salvage operations site and deployed their boom and skimming machinery. Figure 5-1 is an image of the support tug, Awase Maru, demonstrating single ship skimming operations on 3 February. After demonstrating their readiness, the vessels stowed their boom but remained on station, prepared in case an oil spill did occur. The OSR vessels remained on station through the refloating and during the transit to the pier.

Figure 5-1. During the refloating phase, oil response vessels were on the scene in the advent of a fuel spill. This is the support tug Awase Maru with a boom and skimmer deployed demonstrating their readiness should a spill occur.

After refloating, KOCAK proceeded to White Beach and docked at the Navy pier. The ship was encircled with boom at the pier. Once the ship was boomed, the OSR vessels would stand down and return to port.

5-2. Post Salvage Ecological Assessment

After the successful refloating of USNS KOCAK, MSC needed to know the extent of the damage to Ufubishi Reef which USNS KOCAK had struck on 22 January and sat on until 3 February. MSC was very fortunate that no oil had been spilled from the ship but broken sections of coral reef were documented on the video salvage surveys and MSC knew that a detailed investigation was needed. For this they turned to Naval Facilities (NAVFAC) Engineering and Expeditionary Warfare Center's (EXWC) Marine Resource Assessment Diving Services (MRADS). Because Keystone had contracted with an Environmental Response planner, MARENTAS participated alongside MRADS in conducting the reef survey. MARENTAS contracted with Polaris Applied Sciences of Kirkland, WA (USA) which had expertise in coral reef injury assessment to assist in the survey.

The Reef survey was conducted with dives on February 7, 10 and 11 to investigate and document the damage as a result of the grounding. During the total of 730 minutes of combined bottom time, the team evaluated damage inside the KOCAK's footprint and outside the footprint to compare scarred bottom conditions with adjacent unaffected areas. Damage to the reef was observed in four main scars where hull contact resulted in 80 – 100 percent contact damage. This damage can be seen on map provided as Figure 5-2. This map of reef damage, prepared by NAVFAC Marine Resource Assessment Diving Services' Lee Shannon, documents the main scars and the patchy scraped areas likely indicating the hull briefly impacted the coral. The full NAVFAC report is available as Attachment F.

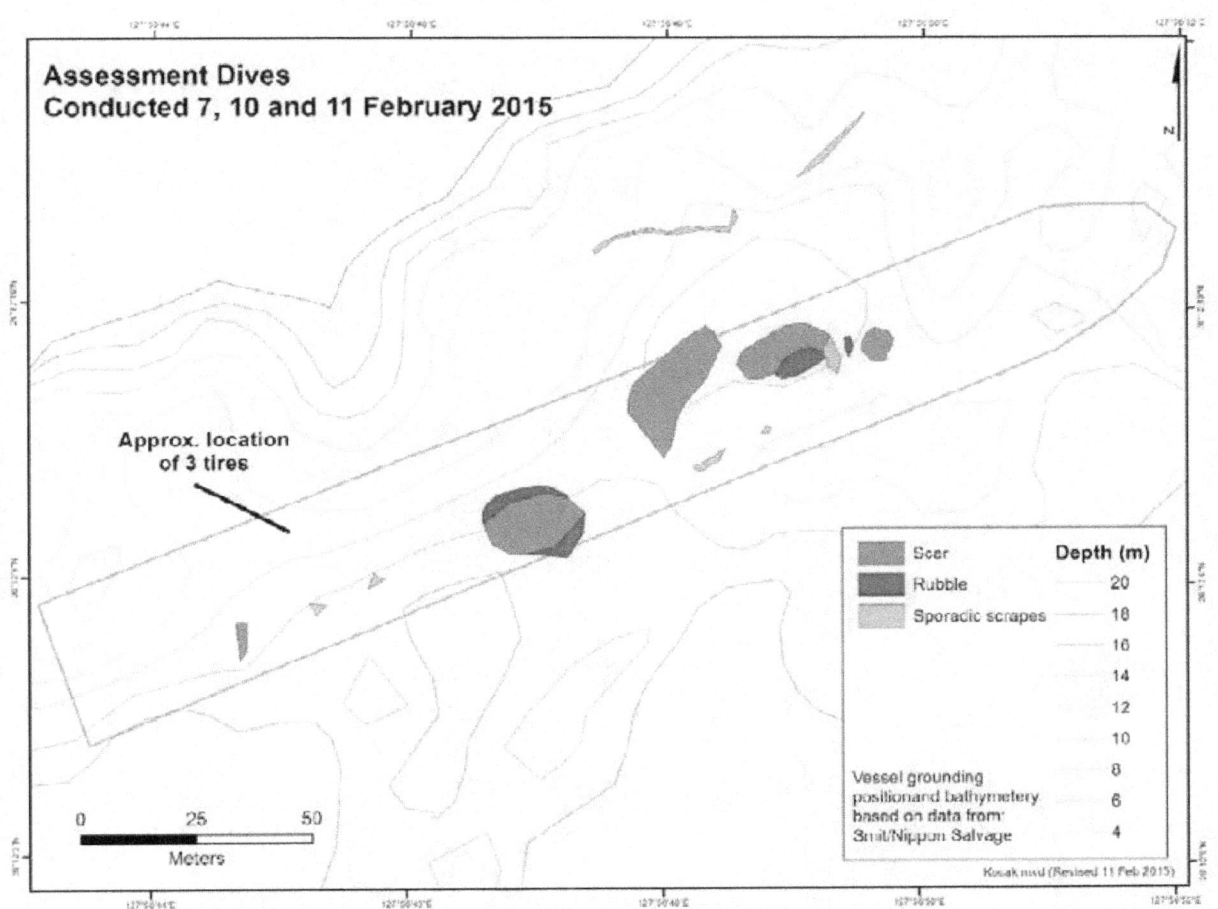

Figure 5-2. Post salvage dive survey map documenting coral damage following KOCAK's extraction.

Potential reef damage in addition to the scaring was evaluated during the survey as well. The areas reviewed were ballast water discharge, dry ballast release, and anti-fouling paint deposits. Conclusions of the assessment team were none of these concerns would result in significant risks or impacts. These conclusions are also documented in the Ecological Assessment Survey Report (Attachment F).

This page intentionally left blank.

6. Conclusion

The conduct of the salvage of USNS SGT MATEJ KOCAK was an unqualified success. There were no personnel injuries; no oil leaks to the sea; no additional damage to the vessel or its cargo as a result of the salvage process; and the refloated vessel was able to steam back to the harbor under its own power. The conduct of salvage operations and damage control efforts while the ship was grounded prevented potential extensive damage to the packed cargo in Holds 4 and 4A and limited damage in Hold 3 (which encountered compartment flooding from 23 – 26 January).

The readiness and capability of the damage control team from USS BONHOMME RICHARD (LHD-6) was a significant factor in limiting damage to the vessel's cargo. The major accomplishments of that team included:

- They were able to dewater all flooded spaces.
- They shored damaged frames in Hold 3A.
- They slowed leaks to manageable level.
- They re-established WT boundary by repairing and reseating door between Holds 3A and 4.

By 5 February the KOCAK response organization was evolving and shifting focus away from ship salvage and onto performing temporary ship repairs, conducting ammo and general cargo offload, conducting a reef survey and public affairs. SUPSALV had ordered a SUPSALV Underwater Ships Husbandry engineer to lead a team from Phoenix International, SUPSALV's underwater operations contractor, to support temporary repair of KOCAK. These were completed in relatively short order and met with the expectation/requirements of USCG and an ABS Inspector.

SUPSALV and the extended capabilities provided by its existing contractors provided Military Sealift Command with a one stop solution to refloating KOCAK and putting her on track toward getting back into service.

This page intentionally left blank.

7. Lessons Learned

SUPSALV considers the debeaching of USNS KOCAK to be a very successful operation. Hence, no major lessons were learned the hard way. Details which were put in play turned out well and this section identifies those successes. We also note areas that will still need to be perfected.

Functional Organization: MSC Chief of Staff on site formed team that incorporated expertise from full range of players. This matrix organization as opposed to a stove pipe organization worked well. It allowed each member to work with their counterpart and provide the best, coordinated service.

Environmental Preparedness Responsibility: The Navy intended to conduct the salvage of KOCAK but expected ship's operator, Keystone, to be responsible for, and put in place a plan, to respond to any environmental issues. Keystone in coordination with The North of England P&I Association Limited (P&I Club) reached out to EMC to arrange for an OSRO to develop and implement an environmental response plan. With these organizations working together, environmental response teams were brought on site in advance of any oil spill and provided Japanese Coast Guard with security of environmental response capability on site during lightening/refloating operations. This also relieved SUPSALV/MSC with providing environmental response team.

On-Site Legal Advice: SEA 00C deployed their Admiralty Attorney to Commander Fleet Activities Okinawa (CFAO) White Beach who interacted with MSC Attorneys to ensure SUPSALV's position and responsibilities were clearly represented. With the complications associated with a Navy Asset which is commercially operated, this turned out to be a good investment in time and assets.

POSSE / NAV ARCH Lessons Learned: POSSE was extremely accurate once adjusted for actual loads vice reported loads (cargo and liquid). The challenge of rapidly obtaining accurate pre- and post-casualty loadings is a well-known but still regularly occurring concern for all salvage operations. The large POSSE files resulted in some file management issues. File backups and sharing was complicated when file size exceeded 50MB.

Waste Oil Management: The ability to pump oily waste to CFAO's waste oil containment barge allowed the pumping down of the flooded spaces and access to the leaks from the inside where temporary patches could be applied. With White Beach Naval Station just 6 miles away, KOCAK's salvor's benefited from the availability of the waste oil containment barges. During periods when the seas increased and a barge could not remain alongside, water levels rose in the damaged spaces and would have become a more significant issue if conditions did not improve.

Transparency with USCG, ABS, and Japanese Coast Guard Reaped Benefits. When developing a repair plan after KOCAK was refloated, the SUPSALV/MSC/Phoenix team brought American Bureau of Shipping (ABS) and U.S. Coast Guard representatives as well as the Japanese Coast Guard personnel on site and tested repair solution ideas in their presence ensuring the final proposed solution would be acceptable within their organizations. This allowed the team to proceed with confidence with their proposed solution before final approvals had been received.

Pre-positioned hull repair equipment staged in Sasebo, Japan provided cost and time savings to the repair process. SUPSALV's Emergency Ship Salvage Material (ESSM) base in Sasebo is stocked with salvage and UWSH equipment which proved useful to the repair process and saved transport time and cost having it already in-country. The ESSM system, with 8 warehouse facilities, provide a ready source of equipment for world-wide casualty response and allows SUPSALV to provide complete turnkey repair solutions.

USNS SGT MATEJ KOCAK
Liquid Offload Plan

30 January 2015

Attachment A

Fuel Transfer

- MSC has tasked the small tanker SLNC PAX to receive fuel from the KOCAK.

- The selection of Diesel Oil tanks to be lightered has been made with considerations towards regaining buoyancy, preserving stability, and limiting the risk to the environment.

- Approximately 10,000 bbl of Diesel Oil will be offloaded from:
  - Wing Tanks #3 P/S
  - Inboard Double Bottom Tanks #4 P/S
  - Inboard Double Bottom Tanks #4A P/S

- FO transfer system is capable of 1000 bbl/hr.

- Once complete, transfers will be secured.

Fuel Transfer Details

- The day prior to the refloat the PAX will transit to KOCAK for transfer of Diesel Oil.
- Tanks to be offloaded in P/S pairs.
- Ballast to be added to #5 Double Bottom Ballast Tanks to offset removed fuel.

Ballast Offload Plan

Comp	Mat'l	Vol (bbl)	Vol (gal)
WING TNK #3S	F76	1112	46704
DBTK#4P INBD	F76	1573	66066
DBTK#4S INBD	F76	1662	69804
DBTK#4AP INB	MGO	2427	101934
DBTK#4AS INB	MGO	2427	101934

SALT WATER BALLAST REMOVAL

- Stern draft will be limited to prevent the propeller and rudder from impacting the reef.

- Day of refloat ballast added to #5 tanks will be offloaded.

- Compressed air will be used to dewater the damaged Outboard Double Bottom Tanks #4 P/S.

- The #5 Wing Tanks P/S will be used to control list and to heel KOCAK to port and off the starboard pinnacle if necessary.

- Ballast water will be removed from the Forepeak Tank to raise bow.

4

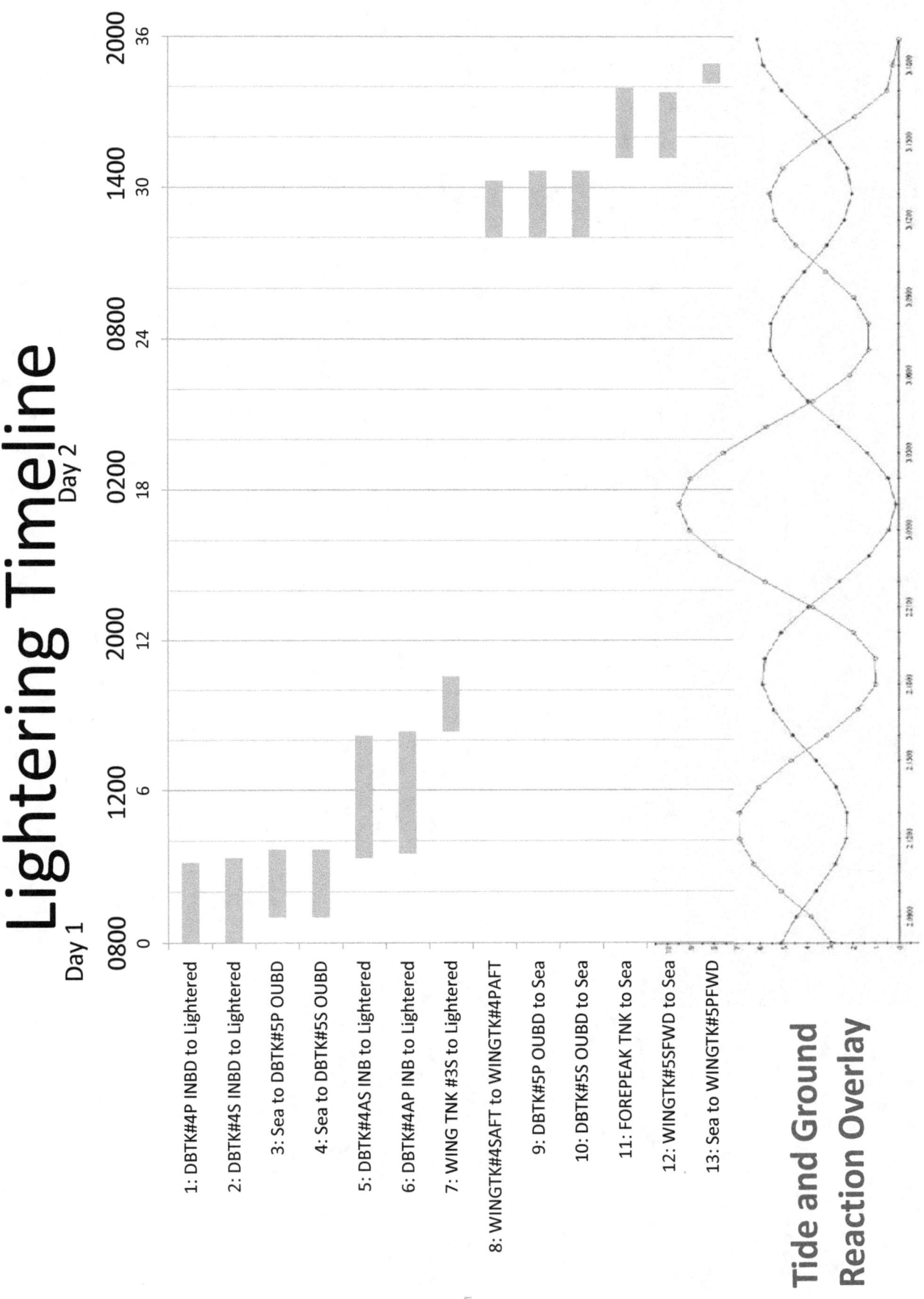

Refloat Schedule

Saturday 31 January

Time	Event
1200	MDPC OSRO already on standby
1300 - 1600	Load Mishima (hoses and fenders)
1700	Move Mishima to mooring

Sunday 1 February

0600	SLNC PAX arrives Nakagusuka Bay
1200	Remove Slop Barge
1400	Move Mishima alongside Kocak
1600	Rig hoses from Kocak across Mishima
1600	Preliminary Go / No-Go decision

Monday 2 February

Time	Event
0500	Go / No-Go decision
0615	SLNC PAX Underway from pier
0830	SLNC PAX moves alongside Mishima
0945	Begin pumping DFM/JP5
1615	Completed pumping planned tanks. Continued pumping to remove add'l 300 tons fuel.
1815	Secure fuel offload

Tuesday 3 February

Time	Event
0200	Move SLNC PAX from Kocak
0700	Last Go/No go decision to commence lightering for float.
	Authorization and acceptance to proceed exists between Stader and Jordan.
0900	Commence discharge sequence as per NAVSEA Jarecki
0930	Pumping stopped due to oil small sheen in water. Restarted pumping after validating source.
0800 - 1200	Ready ship for STBD side stern in docking. Heave anchor-Deck gang responsibility
1200	Position tugs in three key positions. LOGREQ/PREREQ for three tugs to be submitted to MSCO Okinawa for arriving port.
1200	Harbor and docking pilot on board for tug communication purposes only and also to save picking him up on the way in
1300	Abandon ship drill and instruction for all non-crewmembers IVO life raft stations (Menendez/Cadet)
1400	Pre-Float maneuvering conference with Harbor Pilot, Smit Rep, and Master
1550	Cast off Mishima (Nippon Salvage Barge)
1600	Test Gear for getting underway
1600	Escape trunk orientation for DC teams- (Menendez)

Tuesday 3 February (Continued)

Time	Event
1647	Begin pulling astern – two tugs (aprox 100 tons bollard pull)
1730	KOCAK floats Free
	Once clear of after markers, all tugs pull vessel to open water leading with port quarter (tug and thruster power only)
	Turn vessel to White Beach, turn Conn to Harbor Pilot (ship's power, tug power, thruster power)
1800 - 1930	Dead Slow transit to White Beach to allow for best case trim if no flooding exists
1930	Swing vessel to berth stern in starboard side to.
1942	First line to pier
1940 - 2100	Docking
2115	Install Boom around KOCAK
2330 - 2400	Land slop barge, connect hose, and resume discharging slops from cargo holds

Pollution Prevention Contingency Plan

USNS SGT. MATEJ KOCAK (T-AK 3005)
Grounding off Okinawa, Japan,
22 January 2015

Submitted: 31 January 2015
Prepared for: Keystone Shipping Company

USNS SGT. MATEJ KOCAK - Grounding off Okinawa - Japan, 22 January 2015
Pollution Prevention Contingency Plan

Table of Contents

Executive Summary:

In the morning of Thursday 22 January 2015 at approximately 11:30 on an ebb tide, MATEJ KOCAK grounded on a reef off the East Coast of Okinawa, Japan. The vessel is hard aground on a coral reef with a 1.5° port list. There is significant damage to the hull with holds #3A, #4A and #4 flooded. However, various surveys have indicated that the fuel tanks are not breached with the hull nor are they connected to the open sea. There has been no oil loss to the sea observed to date. However, in the aftermath of the grounding and resulting damage, there are certain fuel tanks carrying Diesel Fuel Marine (DFM) which remain vulnerable if not removed prior to refloating. A most likely scenario of 200 - 400 MT (1,335 – 2,670 gallons) (one or two tanks being lost) was considered when drafting the pollution prevention plan. In a spill case scenario, prevailing winds are likely to carry any oil lost into Nakagusuku Bay where resources vulnerable to oil pollution include power plant water intakes, aquaculture (namely seaweed culture) and fishery resources.

To manage the risks due to loss of fuel from the vessel the contingency plan has been prepared drawing upon oil spill response resources available in Okinawa. The location of the casualty is judged too exposed to permit fixed booms to be deployed and the boom anchors would risk further damage to the reef. The proposed solution consists of a containment and recovery response measure, where boom is deployed from a tug and workboat pair as the main defence, with a flexible single ship system to back it up. An Oil Spill Response Organisation (OSRO): the Maritime Disaster Prevention Center (MDPC) has been identified with this capability and a contract has been signed with these.

The vessel remains stable at present and given the proximity of the OSRO's base to the casualty, the OSRO (MDPC) is on standby ready to deploy at short notice. Once the refloating operation commences the equipment will be deployed on the water and will remain on site until the vessel is afloat. The two recovery systems will then follow the vessel as she moves to the USN White Beach berth. At the berth the vessel will be encircled with boom to prevent any oil escape during repairs prior to transfer to dry dock.

1 Background

1.1   Circumstances of the incident

In the morning of Thursday 22 January 2015 at approximately 11:30 on an ebb tide, MATEJ KOCAK grounded at 26°12'1.00"N 127°56'7.00"E. (USNS SGT MATEJ KOCAK,   Length x Breadth: 250.2 m X 32.2 m, Flag: USA (US), MMSI: 366203000, Call Sign: NKCK, Owners: US NAVY (Military Sealift Command), Operators: US Transportation Command (Transcom), Managers: Keystone, P&I Club: North of England). MATEJ KOCAK is a converted RO-RO container ship (Ex. Name: SS JOHN B. WATERMAN), delivered to MSC in the mid 1980s where an insert was introduced in the ship midsection.

MATEJ KOCAK is a government owned vessel operated by Keystone for Military Sealift Command (MSC) under Transcom. When leaving Okinawa, MATEJ KOCAK is reported to be have been carrying liquid cargo: 280 MT (73,968 gal.) of JP5, 2464 MT (650,915 gal.)of F76 Diesel Fuel Marine (DFM), 246 MT (64,986 gal.) Diesel and ~56 MT (14,794 gal.) lube oils (hydraulic oil), distributed as Table 1 below.

Table 1. Distribution of cargo and fuel onboard MATEJ KOCAK when leaving Okinawa on 22 January 2015.

Liquid Cargo: JP5	MT	Gal.
#2 Wing Tank Port	140	36,984
#2 Wing Tank SB	140	36,984
Diesel Fuel Marine (DFM)		
#4A Wing Tank Port	366	96,686
#4A Wing Tank SB	608	160,615
#3 Wing Tank Port	148	39,097
#3 Wing Tank SB	266	70,269
#3 DB Tank Port	120	31,700
#3 DB Tank SB	193	50,985
#4 DB Tank Port	126	33,285
#4 DB Tank SB	201	53,098
#4A DB Tank Port	168	44,381
#4A DB Tank SB	268	70,798
Diesel Oil Tanks		
Diesel Oil Storage	246	64,986

More detailed information was provided by the First Engineer on the above: Diesel Fuel Marine (DFM), which is here Marine Gas Oil (Boiling point: 160 °C, Specific Gravity: 0.840 – 0.880 @ 15.5 °C, Vapour Pressure: 0.4 mm Hg @ 18.3 °C, Vapour Density (air = 1:) 4.7, Viscosity: 1.2 – 4.6 CST @ 37.7 °C, negligible solubility in water, Pour point: -23.3 °C, Flash point: > 60°C, Lower Flammability Limit (% by volume): 0.7, Upper Flammability Limit (% by volume): 5.0, appearance: straw coloured liquid with a hydrocarbon odour).

The liquid cargo, carried in the #2 Wing Tanks, is JP5 (UN: 1203, NATO: F-44) which is a kerosene-based jet fuel. There are approximately 280 MT aboard located in #2 Wing Tanks. JP5 is a yellow kerosene-based jet fuel developed mainly used in aircraft stationed aboard aircraft carriers, where the risk from fire is particularly great. Specific Gravity 0.8, a high flash point (min. 60 °C), freezing point of −46 °C and Vapour pressure of 25 mm Hg.

MATEJ KOCAK is carrying a cargo of several military assets including helicopters, trucks, 4x4 vehicles, humvees, etc. over three decks. It is understood that some of the vehicles operate on JP8 and some of that fuel remains in the vehicles. In addition, MATEJ KOCAK is carrying ordinance cargo onboard.

1.2 Situation of the vessel

After the grounding a fire occurred onboard in Hold #3A, an investigation is ongoing, at this stage it is understood that a humvee battery caught on fire. At the time of grounding, 38 civilian mariners, 26 Marines (USMC) and 67 Soldiers were onboard. None were injured. There have been no reports of oil in the water outside the vessel.

The vessel is hard aground with a 1.5° port list. The vessel is on a reef, touching bottom at three locations with a large part aground alongside a shelf 2/3 forward. The casualty has forward part and aft part afloat.

As of 30 January, a gash (at its widest is 30m / 1 foot) is running between SB Frames 57 – 42 (Cargo Hold #3 & #4, DB Wing Tanks #4 & #3, containing saltwater and fixed ballast respectively) to the bilge ballast tanks. PS frame 52 is damaged; there are three leaks on the PS, one hole (10-12 cm in diameter) and two vertical cracks connecting with the deck. There is flooding in hold #3A, #4 and #4A. Oily water is found in the holds, in particular #3A. It is assumed that there is a leak in the fixed ballast tank PS and that there is a connection between the #3 DB Port Inboard Fuel tank into this tank, but that #3 DB Port is not breached with the hull nor is it connected to the open sea. All other fuel tanks remain intact and none are believed to be in contact with the open sea. It is believed that hold #3A is leaking into hold #4. The leaking in hold #4A is from a breach in the fixed ballast.

From 26 January onwards a 400 ton barge KANTOR 52 has been lightering slops from the flooded holds. KANTOR 52 has an oil / water separator onboard which allows for longer periods of time she can remain moored alongside MATEJ KOCAK for lightering operations. There are another two barges on standby available for lightering. However, lightering has regularly been interrupted as a result of the bad weather and consequent swell. On 26 January all of the #3 DB FO Tanks have successful been transfer into #4 DB's. Plugging of the hull has been undertaken onboard and has reduced flow rate. Two tug vessels are moored to MATEJ KOCAK along her portside, at-times towing and / or standing-by ready to tow in case of emergency. On 1 February tanker PAX is estimated to arrive onsite and begin fuel lightering operations. For further more specific details on the situation of the vessel and salvage operations please refer to specialist reports.

2. Spill risk

The risk of losing JP5 in wing tanks is low as a result of its high location relative to the vessel baseline. In a spill scenario, JP5 would evaporate moderately quickly, F76 will not evaporate as quickly and depending on weather conditions could potentially hit the nearby shoreline.

With regards to the DFM F76, the risk from #3 Wing and #4A Wing are considered low when taking into account their position on the vessel. #3 Wing position is 2.5m (8 feet) above the vessel tank tops and #4A located at tank top level.

#3 DBs have been pumped into #4 DB. #4 DB and #4A DB fuel oil tanks remain vulnerable during any further movement of the vessel on the reef leading to a most likely scenario of up to some 200 - 400 MT (1,335 - 2,670 gallons) (one or two tanks being lost) during salvage operations, if not removed prior to refloating. Removing all the fuel from these tanks is part of the lightering plan (please refer to specialist reports for further details). Once the fuel has been removed, the pollution risk is greatly reduced leaving only a minimal amount of residual 'clingage' in the lightered double bottom fuel tank. DFM will be retained in the Diesel Oil Storage tanks for ships service and propulsion and. DFM will also be retained in the # 4A Wing Tanks (P&SB) for stability and trim. There is no indication that any of these tanks are at risk.

3. Characterises of the area and sensitive resources

Okinawa Prefecture is the southernmost prefecture of Japan. It is composed of hundreds of the Ryukyu Islands in a chain over 1,000 kilometres (620 miles) long, extending south-westerly towards Taiwan. Okinawa's capital, Naha is located in the southern part of Okinawa Island where the main international airport is located, a 1.5 hour drive to Nakagusuku Port.

MATEJ KOCAK ran aground off the East Coast of Okinawa, in the eastern portion of Nakagusuku Bay. This bay is located on the southern coast of Okinawa Island. The bay covers 220 km^2 (137 miles^2) with an average depth of 15m (50 feet). It contains two islands Kudaka Island and Tsuken Island. Tatsu Kuchi is the main sea entrance into the bay; it is 3 km (2 miles) wide and has a depth of 55m (180 feet). Numerous large and small islands, reefs, and shoal waters bracket the entrance.

Okinawa is home to a variety of fauna and flora including the endangered marine mammal, the dugong and sea turtles which lay their eggs in the southern islands of Okinawa. Okinawa and the many islands that make up the Prefecture contain some abundant coral reefs. The incident area is known for coral reefs and coral has been observed in the immediate vicinity of the vessel. Two fishing villages are in the vicinity of the casualty: Iheiya and Awase.

The closest point to landfall is less than 5 km (2.8 miles) away from the grounding site.

The general location of Nakagusuku Bay is composed of a combination of man-made structures, seaweed cultivation facilities, sandy beaches, rocky outcrops and LNG / LPG and oil refinery facilities. From information collected onsite, from boat surveys, desk-based research and collected verbally from local sources: the following information has been collated:

- The vessel ran aground off the outer NW edge of Uhu Bisi reef which stretches over 5 km (3 miles) in a NW – SE direction forming an inverted C curve, with a width ranging from 1 – 2 km (0.6 – 1.2 miles) wide.

- Tsuken Island, at the entrance of Nakagusuku Bay, is immediately north of the grounding location and would be the closet point (5 km / 2.8 miles) to landfall in case of an incident (with southerly winds). Tsuken covers ~2 km^2 (1.3 miles^2) and has a population of some 500 residents. Tsuken is composed of white sand beaches and a broad coral reef. The island has three small hotels and a campground. The economy relies on tourism and farming. Around this island lie seaweed-farms (nori and mozuku culture)

- On the NE end of the bay, along the southern tip of the Katsuran Peninsula is located the US White Beach Naval Port Facility. The White Beach Navy Ammunition Pier and White Beach Army Pier extend into Nakagusuku Bay.

- Travelling westwards from White Beach Naval Port, the coastline is composed of a combination of sandy beach, manmade structures and rocky shoreline around to the Nakagusuku port. At the entrance of Nakagusuku Bay, immediately adjacent to the antennae lie seaweed farms.

- Continuing around the bay anticlockwise, the coastline is industrialised and manmade. LNG Okinawa Electric Power plant, is situated opposite the Maritime Disaster Prevention Center (MDPC) Oil Spill Response (OSR) warehouse.

- Further along lies the Nansei Sekiyu oil refinery, which produces gasoline, diesel, fuel oil, jet fuel, light oil, and oil derivatives, for Petróleo Brasileiro S.A. – Petrobras subsidiary.

- Further along in the next bay is located the LPG Berth Marui Gas.

- In addition to the above industrial structures, Nakagusuku Bay contains seaweed, angler fishing and aquaculture facilities (fish and shrimp).

- No mangroves are found in Nakagusuku Bay, these are located in areas further north and west of Okinawa.

Please refer to Appendix 6.2. and 6.3. for further details on local sensitivities.

4. Response arrangements

4.1 General arrangements
In Japan, it is the Japanese Coastguard (JCG) that has the mandate to investigate and respond to oil spill incidents. It is the lead agency for salvage and spill response but looks to shipowners to undertake cleanup operations. After notification of a major potential or actual spill, the JCG would typically dispatch vessels and/ or aircraft to assess the situation. The shipowner is required to take emergency or damage control measures and clean up the spill. If it is deemed that the incident exceeds the shipowner's capability, the Marine Disaster Prevention Centre (MDPC), funded jointly by government and industry, will respond either under the direction of the JCG or under direct contract with the Owner. In addition, there are also substantial quantities of privately held response equipment at oil receiving facilities, by private contractors or through MDPC and the Petroleum Association of Japan (PAJ). Tripartite councils involving government, local and private sector representatives have been established at ports & harbours to promote contingency planning and consider equipment

requirements. The Ports & Harbours Departments of the Ministry of Transport is responsible for guidance and disposal.

Japanese policy focuses on physical containment and recovery, anticipating the majority of oil will be recovered with skimmers and nets. The remainder recovered with sorbents pads or chemically dispersed. Dispersants usage must first be approved by JCG and with the agreement of the local Fishermen's Cooperative. Dispersant use is increasingly rare in Japan. Disposal of collected oil is usually incinerated, although it may sometimes also be taken for blending or refining if it is in a pure enough form. Contaminated waste may be land filled or incinerated. JCG maintains stocks of equipment and materials through its local branches (information from ITOPF Country Profiles).

4.2 The Response Plan

Here Keystone has been tasked with pollution prevention and response (not salvage). Keystone have received a request from USN to put in place a contingency plan, contract a local Oil Spill Pollution Origination (OSRO) and prepare contingency arrangements to clean up any oil lost from the vessel. ECM and MARENTAS are tasked to help coordinate this. ECM are the contracted US Spill Managers for Keystone and Keystone contracted Natasha Lippens of MARENTAS to attend onsite on ECM behalf.

In Okinawa both MDPC and PAJ have equipment stockpiles and have provided equipment lists and both are ready to respond as required.

After several discussions held with MDPC and PAJ, ECM / MARENTAS recommended the use of MDPC as Oil Spill Response Organisation (OSRO). This is because PAJ only offer equipment, with no personnel, no transport to / from their base in Uruma and no vessels. MDPC offer a one-stop-shop for all these assets and so has been chosen. However, understanding the dynamic nature of the situation, the additional assets offered by PAJ can always be brought in at a later stage, if necessary, and there is room for this in this Contingency Plan.

MDPC own their own equipment and have a longstanding contract with Okinawa Marine Service to act as their local agents as well as provide vessel services. MDPC have been hired by North of England P&I Club one-half of Keystone.

This plan covers oil spill contingency arrangements from the present time, and includes each stage of the operation; float free, the subsequent survey/assessment period up until the vessel is moored at USNS White Beach. The plan has therefore been divided into the following sections for ease of review.

a)   Present time up until refloating stage (including lightering operations)
b)   Refloating stage (float free)
c)   Subsequent survey/assessment period – immediately after refloating
d)   Movement under her own steam to USNS White Beach
e)   Mooring at USNS White Beach, while she undergoes repairs up until she sails of to dry-dock

Natasha Lippens (ECM / MARENTAS) is the POC (Point of Contact) in case of any emergency and based in Okinawa until refloating, normally located at White Beach Command Centre.

The Japanese Coast Guard (JCG) will at all times be kept informed of an incident. During an oil pollution event which places resources in the bay or ashore at risk the JCG would be notified to enable them to advise local stakeholders such at LNG Okinawa Electric Power plant, LPG Berth Marui Gas or the fishermen to protect their water intakes or any other relevant structures. Natasha has an agreement with the local JCG to call them in case of any emergency and JCG have confirmed that they in turn will warn the LNG and oil refinery to deploy their own boom to protect their water intakes, if this is deemed necessary.

a)   Present time up until refloating stage (including lightering operations)
MDPC, the OSRO are placed on standby. They have a base in Nakagusuku Bay, right behind the LNG plant, 7-8nm from the grounding. To-date, equipment has not been deployed as a result of the dynamic conditions on-site and because of the risk of interference with the salvage operation. Currently booms would not be an effective way of corralling or containing any oil released, due to the strong waves and exposed position. Deployed boom is unlikely to hold in such sea conditions thus resulting in damage to any boom deployed and loss of any oil that had been contained.

Fixed booms are not recommended in this context as there has been concern that the anchoring arrangements for the boom would risk causing additional damage to the coral reef. The use of dispersants would not normally be recommended nearby coral and aquaculture facilities as are present here.

Taking the above into account, the following equipment from MDPC is to be placed on standby:

Unit	Item	Description
1	Recovery vessel (all-in-one)	Single Ship Recovery System
1	Skimmer	Foilex mini
1	Outrigger	7m aluminium pole
100m	Recovery boom	'Oil skimming boom'
200m	Boom	inflatable oil boom
1	Tug	Kariyushi (PS 952)
1	Work boat	Type IV (PS 4354) tugs

The tug and workboat form a 'J' configuration to collect and recover any lost oil while the Single Ship Recovery System provides flexibility to recover oil which is not contained by the boom. The tug and workboat form a 'J' configuration using 200m inflatable boom. The operational limits for this arrangement are considered to be wave heights <1 m and currents < 2 knots and Wind speed < Beaufort 4-5.

See Appendix 3 for further details on the Single Ship Recovery System and Appendix 4 for the U Shaped Configuration.

In addition Nippon Salvage have onboard their barge 300m of boom available and 60m onboard HIYASI MARU which are on standby. However, it was considered best to separate salvage and oil pollution response assets.

b)   Refloating stage (float free)

Natasha will be based at White Beach during these operations. MDPC would be deployed to site. Tug and workboat would form a 'J' configuration and recovery vessel would be onsite ready to collect and recover any lost oil.

Please note that if it is decided to conduct the refloat after daylight the risks of operating with towed boom in shallow waters at night together with the dynamic salvage operations and associated vessels, would call for a safety assessment to be conducted prior to the refloat in order to determine if it was best to place MDPC on standby or to deploy them to site.

c) **The subsequent survey/assessment period – immediately after refloating (if conducted)**
Tug and workboat 'J' configuration and recovery vessel would remain onsite, ready to collect and recover any lost oil.

d) **Movement under her own steam to USNS White Beach**
Tug and workboat 'J' configuration and recovery vessel would follow the vessel in, one on portside the other starboard, as navigational safety allows, ready to collect and recover any lost oil.

e) **Mooring at USNS White Beach, while she undergoes repairs**
Once moored to USN East Navy pier at White Beach base, 800m of boom will be used to encircle USNS SGT MATEJ KOCAK (Length x Breadth: 250.2 m X 32.2 m), alongside the pier. This will remain until the risk of oil pollution from the vessel has been removed. The tug and workboat boom, skimmer and recovery vessel configuration would be demobilised if no oil spill has occurred, once the boom is deployed around the vessel. The boom belongs to USN White Beach and will be deployed and monitored by these.

Note: The US Navy has advised that they would make available the use of their helicopter(s) to assist in directing on water containment and recovery operations as required if so requested.

5. Ballast water sampling:

The ship's engineering staff will ensure that samples are taken of any ballast water that will be discharged either as part of the refloating or while alongside at USNS White Beach. The samples will be taken via a sampling valve on the suction side of the ship's ballast pump. Samples will be collected at regular intervals (beginning, middle and end) during the ballast operations.

Best regards,

Natasha Lippens, Okinawa (Japan)
Mobile #: +86 186 21 65 62 57
natasha.lippens@marentas.com

Scott May, Connecticut (U.S.A.)
Mobile #: +1 203 247 1646
scottm@ecmmaritime.com

6.1. Appendix 1: Contact list

Unless otherwise specified as denoted by [*] all contacts speak English. If need be Mr Robert Helton (CNFJ) is 24/7 contactable for translation support (English / Japanese).

Surname	Name	Company	Telephone	Email	Comment
Helton	Robert	CNFJ	(81) 080 42098622	heltonuscsd@gmail.com	Linguist
May	Scott	ECM	(1) 203 247 1646	scottm@ecmmaritime.com	
Hasegawa	Tetsuya	Heisei Shipping	(81) 090 1509 3746	ops@hship.co.jp	Ship Agent
		JCG 24h	118		
		JCG Nakagusuku	(1) 098 938 7118		*
O'Connor	Timothy	Keystone	(1) 484-433-3469	toconnor@keyship.com	
Sashida	Yuji	Kyowa Marine Service Co., Ltd.	(1) 090 9875 0332	y.sashida@km-s.co.jp	PAJ
Lippens	Natasha	MARENTAS / ECM	(86) 186 21 65 62 57	natasha.lippens@marentas.com	POC
		MATEJ KOCAK Bridge	(1) 619 533 7224 (Ext. 3)		
Hideomi	Kakimoto	MDPC	(1) 080 2046 1184	h-kakimoto@mdpc.or.jp	
Togo	Tetsuzo	MDPC	(1) 090 4359 3843	tetu-tougou@btvm.ne.jp	
		MDPC Yokohama Head Office	(1) 045 224 4315		*
Stader	Paul	MSC Chief of Staff	(1) 757 739 9598		
Storz	William	MSC Legal	(1) 202 549 3517	william.storz@navy.mil	
Welborn	Carl	MSC Okinawa Director	(81) 090 9789 9605	carl.welborn@fe.navy.mil	
Ohkubo	Jiro	Nippon Salvage	(81) 080 1719 4306	jiro.okubo@nipponsalvage.co.jp	
Ichikawa	Yoshihisa	Nippon Salvage	(81) 080 1719 4306		
Moloney	Eamon	North of England P&I	(44) 77 11 039 390	eamon.moloney@nepia.com	
				[continue over next page]	

				[continue from last page]	
Hojo	Tomoyuki	PAJ	(81) 080 8749 9439	t.hojo@sekiren.gr.jp	
Wisse	Dave	Smit Salvage	(65) 972 573 30	d.wisse@smit.com	
Duit	Jan Willem	Smit Salvage	(31) 64 604 29 25	j.duit@smit.com	Salvage Master
Baumann	Gregg	SUPSALV	(1) 202 781 0731	gregg.baumann@navy.smil.mil	On-Scene-Commander

6.2. Appendix 2. Overview of local area showing manmade sensitivities

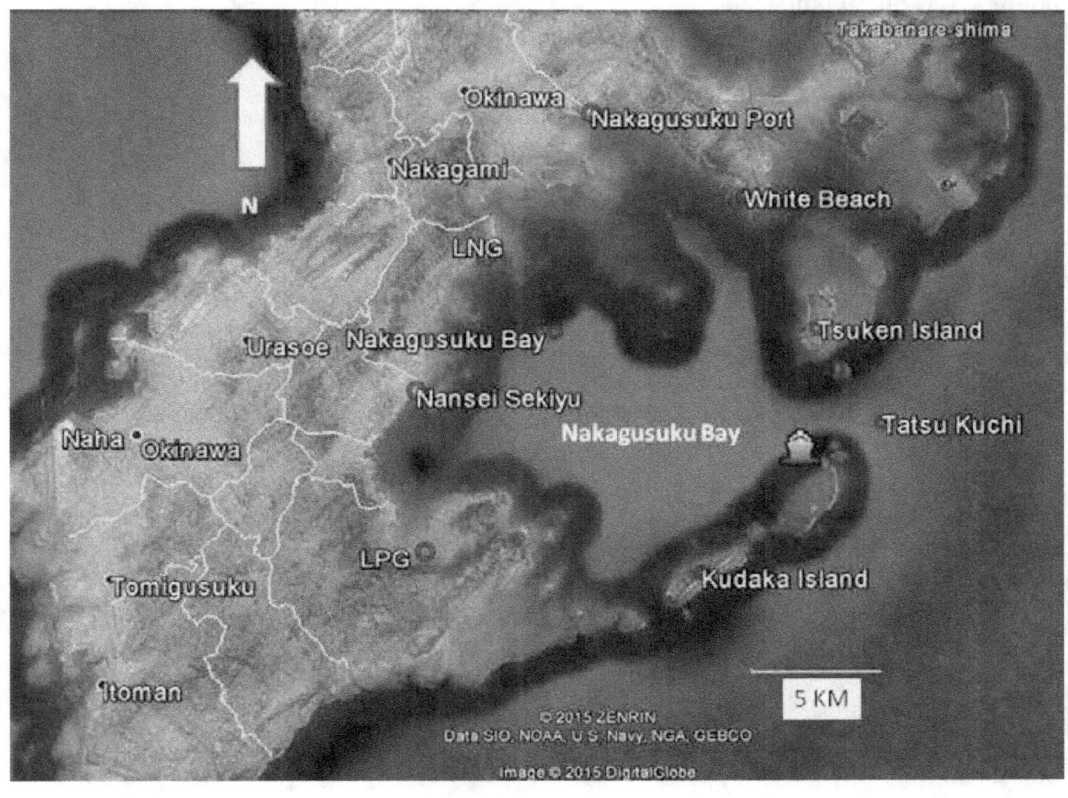

6.3. Appendix 3. Overview of local area showing fishery seaweed culture (shaded in red) (provided by JCG on 30 January).

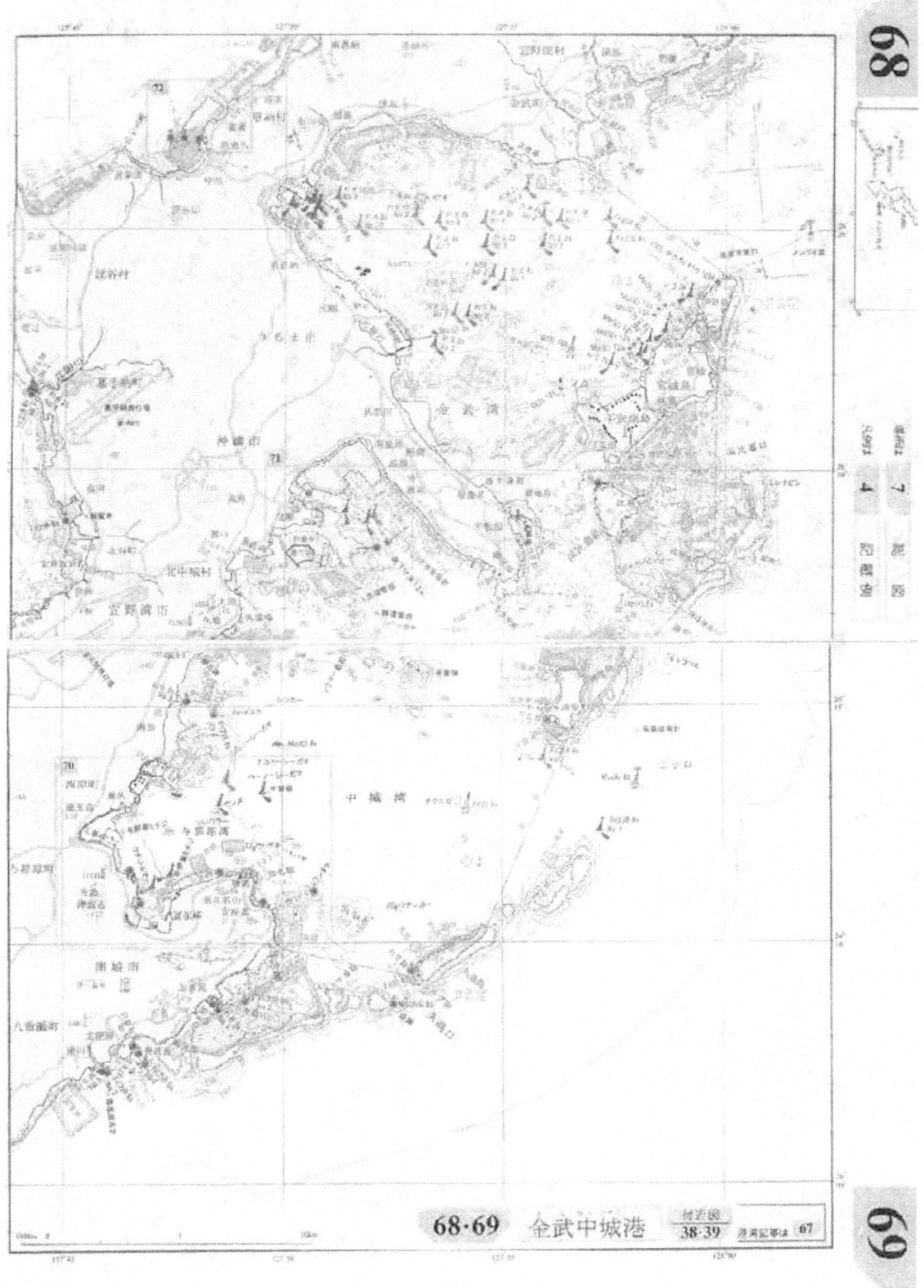

6.4. Appendix 4: Single Ship System

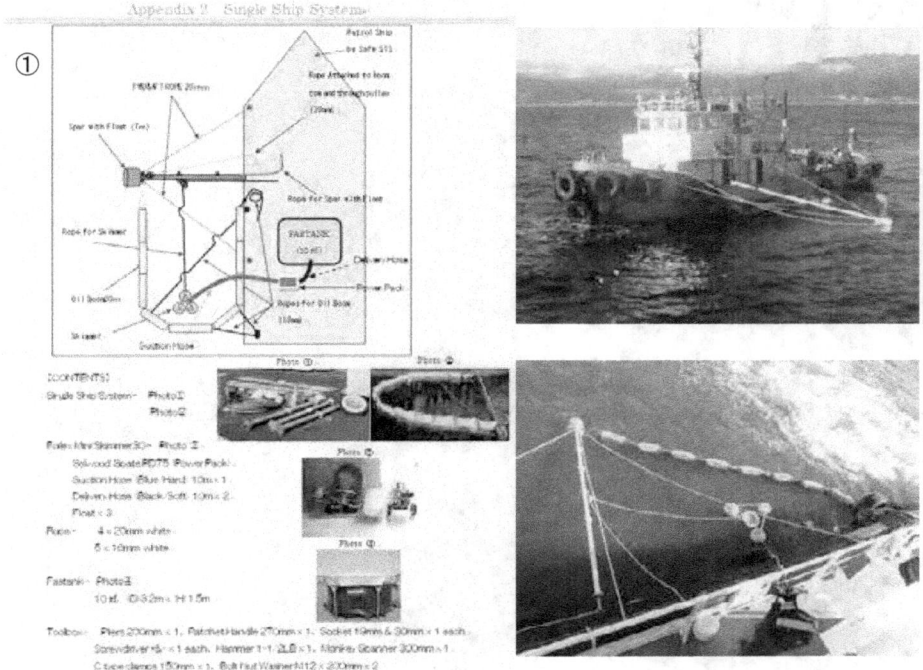

(image courtesy of MDPC)

6.5. Appendix 5. U Shaped Configuration

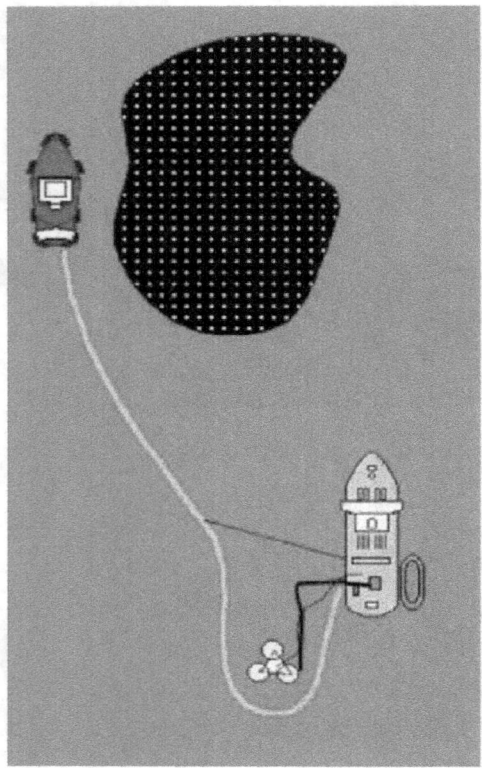

(image courtesy of MDPC)

6.6. Appendix 6. MDPC Equipment Stockpile Available at Nakagusuku Port

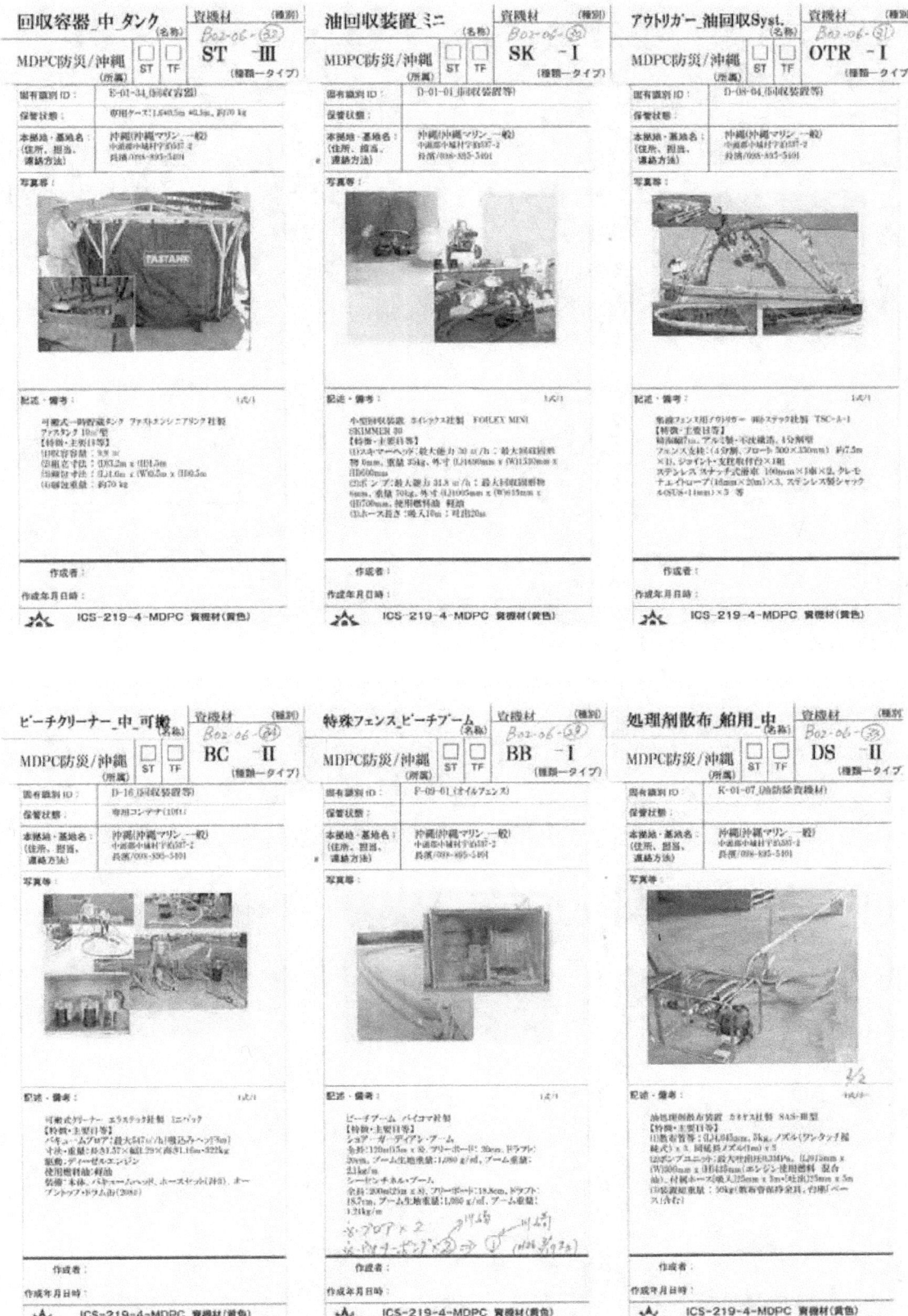

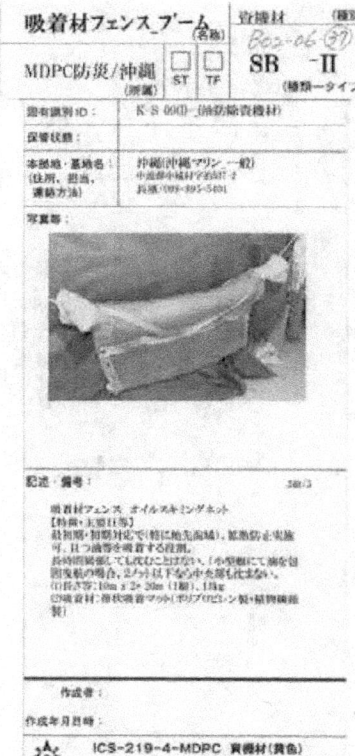

6.7. Appendix 7. Okinawa Marine Service Vessels Available at Nakagusuku Port (working with MDPC)

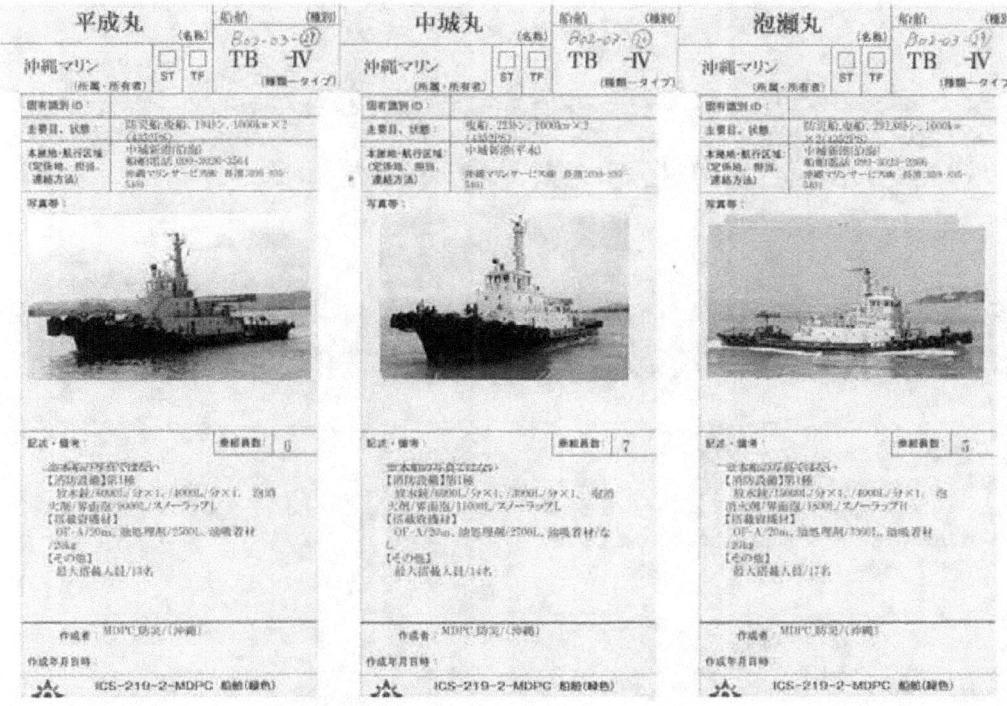

6.8. Appendix 8. PAJ's Oil Spill Response Equipment Stockpile available at Uruma

●国内油濁防除資機材基地(Domestic Equipment Stockpile Bases)

基地名(Base)		第1号 東京湾基地 (Tokyo Bay)	第2号 瀬戸内基地 (Seto Inland Sea)	第3号 伊勢湾基地 (Ise Bay)	第4号 日本海基地 (Sea of Japan)	第5号 北海道基地 (Hokkaido)	第5号 北海道基地 稚内分所 (Wakkanai)	第6号 沖縄基地 (Okinawa)
所在地(Location)		千葉県市原市 (Ichihara)	岡山県倉敷市 (Mizushima)	三重県四日市市 (Yokkaichi)	新潟県新潟市 (Niigata)	北海道室蘭市 (Muroran)	北海道稚内市 (Wakkanai)	沖縄県うるま市 (Uruma)
開設時期(Opening)		平成3年11月 (Nov.'91)	平成4年9月 (Sep.'92)	平成5年3月 (Mar.'93)	平成5年9月 (Sep.'93)	平成6年10月 (Oct.'94)	平成22年7月 (Jul.'10)	平成7年3月 (Mar.'95)
充気式オイルフェンス (Inflatable Boom)	Ro-Boom 1800	500m	500m	500m	500m	500m	–	500m
	Ro-Boom 1800SPI	–	–	–	–	–	250m	–
	Ro-Boom 2200	–	250m	–	–	–	–	–
	Ro-Boom Beach 800+650	–	320m	–	320m	–	–	–
	Deep Sea Boom	250m	500m	500m	500m	250m	–	–
	Hd Sprint Boom	250m	–	–	–	250m	–	500m
	Uni Boom 800R	–	–	–	–	250m	–	–
	Uni Boom X1800	250m	–	–	250m	–	–	–
	Vee Sweep	–	–	60m	60m	60m	–	60m
	Beach Boom (neoprene)	320m	–	320m	–	320m	–	320m
	Current Buster	72m	–	72m	–	–	72m	–
	Current Buster 4	74m	74m	–	–	–	–	–
	Harbour Buster	–	–	–	–	–	–	60m
流出油回収機 (Oil Skimmer)	Lamor LFF 350/140	–	1	–	–	–	–	–
	Transrec 100	–	–	–	1	1	–	–
	Transrec 125	1	–	–	–	–	–	–
	Giant Octopus	–	1	–	–	–	–	–
	URO 300	–	–	–	1	–	–	–
	Desmi Combination Skimmer	3	1	3	2	2	1	3
	GT 185-8	–	2	2	–	–	–	–
	Komara 15 Duplex	–	4	4	4	4	–	–
	Komara 40	–	2	2	–	–	–	2
	Komara 12K	–	–	–	–	–	–	4
	Komara Star	–	2	4	2	2	–	2
	DIP402 VOSS	–	–	1	–	–	–	1
	Lamor LWS 50	2	1	–	2	2	1	–
	TDS 118	2	–	–	2	–	–	–
移送ポンプシステム (Crane Sweep System)		1	1	1	1	1	–	1
ビーチクリーナー (Beach Cleaner)	Mini Vac System	6	6	6	6	6	2	6
回収油バージ (Inflatable Barge)	25t (Lancer Barge)	1	1	1	1	1	1	1
	75t (NOFI Oil Barge)	–	2	–	–	–	–	–
	100t (Lancer Barge)	–	–	–	–	2	–	–
オイルバッグ (Oil Bag)	50t	1	1	1	1	1	–	1
	200t	2	1	–	2	–	–	–
ロータンク (Ro-Tank)	25t	1	1	1	1	1	–	1
仮設タンク (Portable Tank)	1.5t	6	6	6	6	6	2	6
	5t	6	6	6	6	6	2	6
	9t	24	24	24	24	24	6	24
緊急排出ポンプ (Emergency Discharge Pump)		–	–	–	–	1	–	–
油水分離機 (Oily Water Separator)		2	2	2	2	2	–	2
トレルテント (Trelltent)		1	1	1	1	1	–	1
可搬式照明器具 (Portable Lighting System)		2	2	2	2	2	–	2
油揚資材 (Oil Snare)		60袋	60袋	60袋	60袋	60袋	60袋	60袋
ブームベイン (Boom Vane)		1	1	1	1	1	1	1
固形式オイルフェンス (Solid Boom)	Solid 1150	7,040m	4,000m	2,080m	1,920m	1,920m	960m	2,080m
	Boom Bag	200m	200m	200m	200m	200m	–	200m

2014年3月現在
As of March 2014

6号沖縄基地(Okinawa)

5号北海道基地 稚内分所(Hokkaido)

7

USNS SGT MATEJ KOCAK POSSE SALVAGE REPORT

INTRODUCTION

After loading cargo and ammunition for Exercise COBRA GOLD, USNS SGT MATEJ KOCAK (T-AK 3005) ran aground exiting Okinawa harbor on 22 January 2015 at 1110 local time. The grounding caused no personnel injuries or oil pollution. Harbor tugs were summoned to stabilize and attempt to refloat the vessel. KOCAK did not refloat on the next (spring) high tide.

Figure 1: USNS KOCAK Aground

VESSEL DETAILS

USNS KOCAK is a combined container and roll-on/roll-off cargo ship owned by the US Navy's Military Sealift Command operated by contract mariners. KOCAK was delivered to MSC in the mid-1980s after a mid-body extension. She has eight total holds; the forward three are container holds and the aft 5 are RO/RO vehicle holds. Each vehicle hold has six levels including the main (weather) deck.

Particulars
Length: 821 ft
Beam: 106 ft
Displacement: 1,162 tons
Speed: 20 knots
Crew: 25

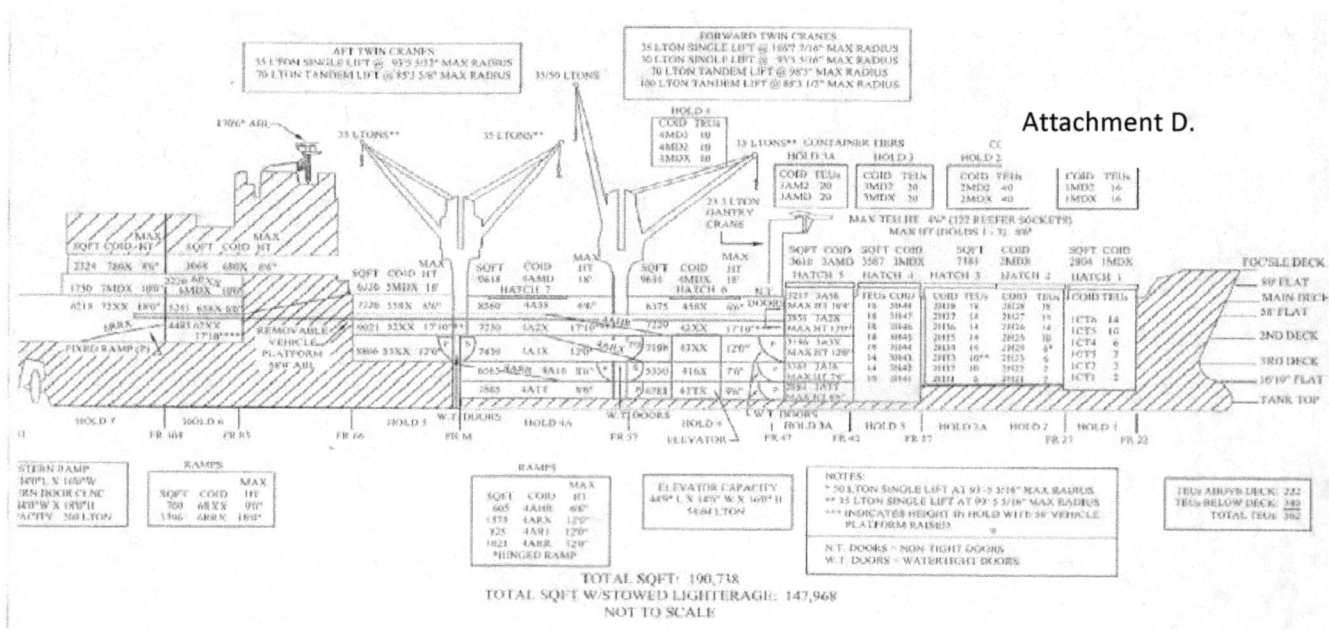

Figure 2: KOCAK Profile and Stowage

2

GROUNDING ASSESSMENT

KOCAK ran aground on Ufu Vishi Reef while exiting White Beach Naval Facility, Okinawa, Japan

Figure 3: Grounding Location

KOCAK was hard aground throughout the tide cycle. Multiple dive surveys were performed to identify ground locations. KOCAK was aground on a coral shelf running diagonally beneath Cargo Holds 4 and 3A (Fig. 4). Additionally, a smaller coral pinnacle was beneath the starboard side forward of the house (not shown). KOCAK was afloat at the bow and stern but clearance below the rudder and propeller was only about 1m. This complicated refloat efforts as additional trim had to be limited.

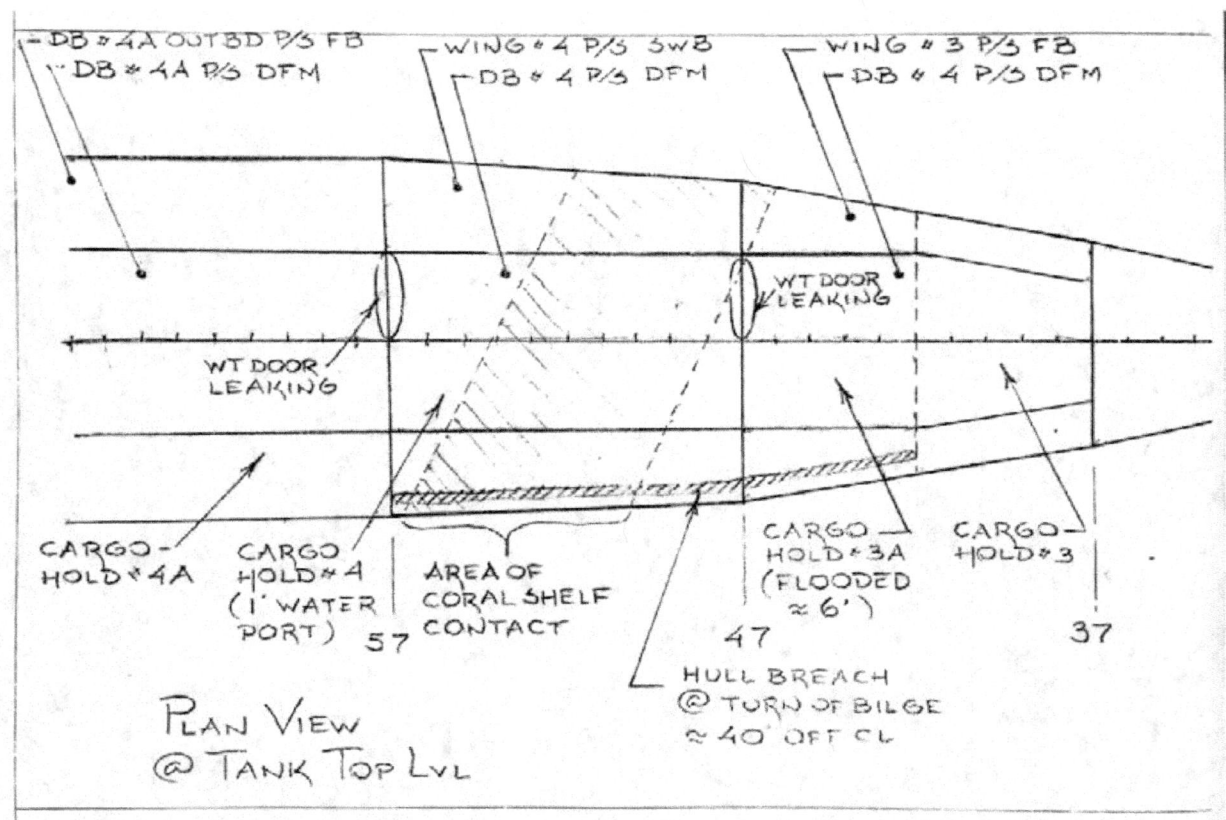

Figure 4: Damage and Grounding Location

Figure 5: Propeller Clearance

4

Ground reaction calculations estimated KOCAK aground by approximately 3000 LT at high tide 26 February (5.7-ft above MLLW) and 10,000 LT at low tide (1.5-ft above MLLW). List was always to port at approximately 1.5 degrees. Vessel was lively enough to roll slightly at high tide but static at low tide.

A bathymetric survey was performed in the area around KOCAK. In addition to identifying a shallow coral outcropping to port even with the deckhouse the survey showed clear water astern and guided the extraction route.

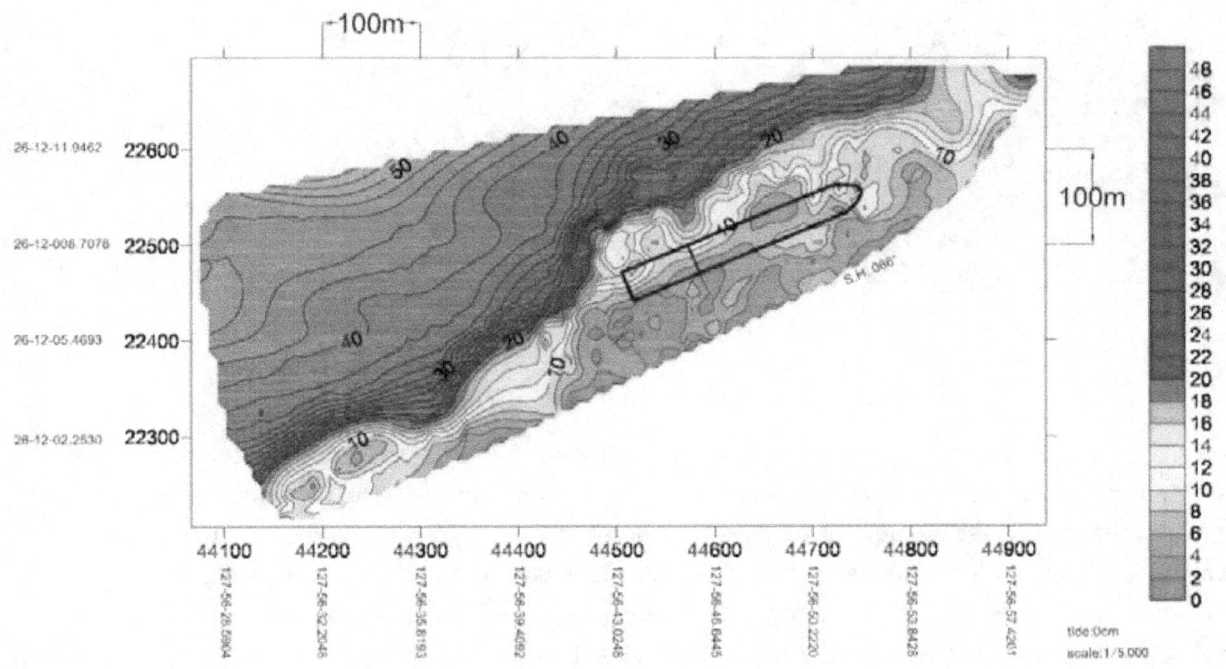

Figure 6: Bathymetric Survey

DAMAGE ASSESSMENT

External damage identified during dive surveys consisted solely of a longitudinal breach of the starboard hull plating running from the forward of Frame 57 to aft of Frame 42. Hull damage ran below the bilge keel and penetrates ballast tanks 4S Outboard and 3S Outboard. No fuel tanks were breached. No external hull damage was visible on the port side but KOCAK was heavily aground along that side hindering survey efforts.

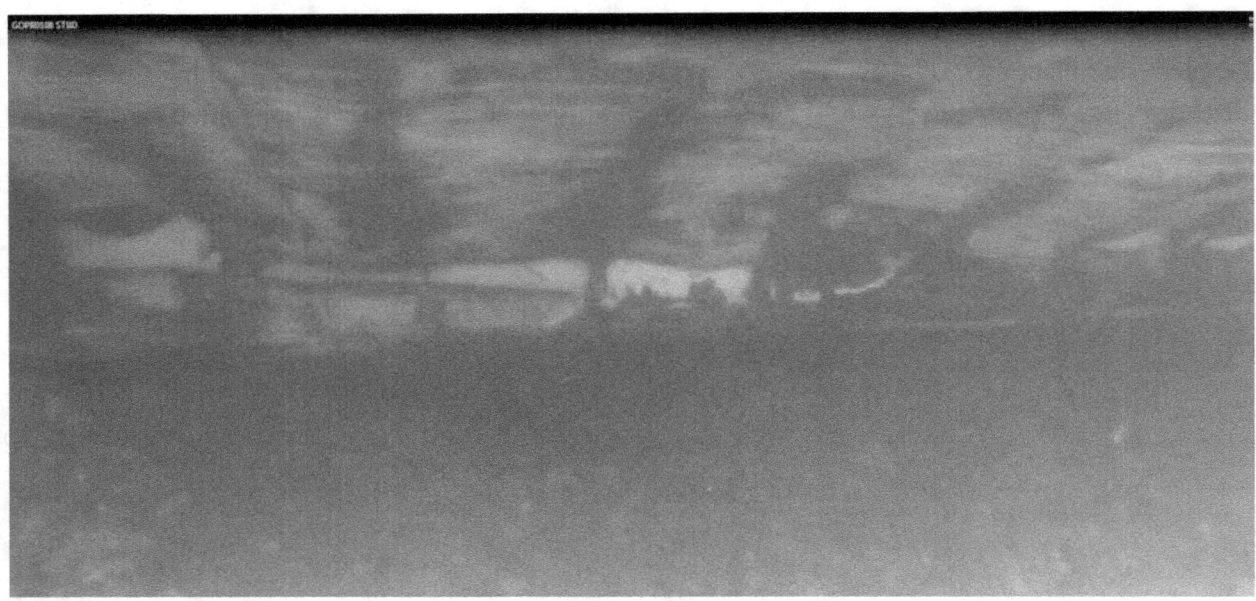

Figure 7: Hull Damage (Stbd)

Internal damage consisted of seawater flooding into Cargo Hold 3A. On 23 January the floodwater reached and ignited an unsecured battery in one of the cargo vehicles. The fire was extinguished and the hold secured. Over the next three days the floodwater in Cargo Hold 3A rose to approximately 6-ft which was below the waterline and indicated a slow leak rather than complete free communication. The lower deck watertight vehicle doors on the port side between Cargo Holds 3A and 4 and Cargo Holds 4 and 4A were forced out of alignment allowing floodwater to progress from Cargo Hold 3A into Cargo Holds 4 and 4A.

With assistance from a Damage Control team from the USS BONHOMME RICHARD (LHD-6) all three flooded holds were pumped dry to a slop barge alongside. Water ingress was identified only in hold 3A on the port side and was secured save for one leak forward of FR 47 which was manageable throughout the refloat. Floodwater was coming into Hold 3A through the #3 Outboard Port Double Bottom tank which is filled with a permanent ballast powder of primarily iron. Fuel levels in the adjoining 3P Wing and 3P Inboard DB were unchanged. Structural damage occurred to Frame 45 on the port side of the hold level of Cargo Hold 3A buckling approximately 6 inches. The web but not flange of the two frames to either side of Frame 45 also buckled approximately 3 inches. Additionally, the welds connecting Frames 44-46 to the 3 Stbd Wing Tank above cracked to varying degrees. Damage Control teams shored both sides of Frame 45 to prevent further buckling damage and the cracks were monitored for propagation.

Figure 8: Frame 45 Damaged & Shored

Additional structural damage was identified as cargo hold tank top decks forced upward along a longitudinal girder running through the double bottom tanks 9 ft inboard of the port bulkhead in Cargo Holds 3A and 4. The deck in this area is raised from 2-5 inches. This resulted in the misalignment of the vehicle doors and buckling of a longitudinal between FR 44 and 45 on the port side of Cargo Hold 3A. Watertight integrity was re-established in the door between Hold 3A and 4 but the door between Hold 4 and 4A continued to leak by even with DC plugs and epoxy patches applied.

Figure 9: Dislodged Watertight Door

Structural damage, while not insignificant, was not considered to be a driving factor in refloating the KOCAK. An extremely conservative analysis assuming that all potentially damaged longitudinal members were completely ineffective resulted in an 8% reduction is total sectional area at the most heavily damaged location. Efforts were made to limit stresses on the hull but not at the expense of attaining the proper buoyancy and attitude to refloat.

INITIAL POSSE ANALYSIS

POSSE MODEL

The NAVSEA Supervisor of Salvage (SUPSALV) maintains Program of Ship Salvage Engineering (POSSE) models for all US Navy vessels, combatant and auxiliary. The model for KOCAK included an .shp ship model and four .smd section modulus files. The .shp file was compared to the current Trim and Stability Book and found to accurately match the vessel as currently outfitted.

VESSEL LOADING

Accurate pre-stranding weights and drafts are crucial for developing a plan to refloat a vessel. While the total vessel displacement largely matched the departure condition provided from KOCAK's CargoMax loading computer some discrepancies were discovered. In order to ensure the most accurate starting point for refloating KOCAK all tanks were manually sounded and compared to the engine room tank level indicators. This gave an indication of which TLI's may not be accurate. Additionally, there was substantial confusion as to the total weight and center of cargo vehicles onboard. The Army Loadmaster responsible for all vehicle cargo developed from his inventory a detailed list of cargo weights broken down into the Integrated Computerized Deployment System (ICODES) categories based on hold and deck level. A Detailed Weight in POSSE was used to consolidate these individual point loads into a single weight without losing the disparate centers of gravity. Weight discrepancies included approximately 400-LT less DFM than reported but greater than 500-LT more cargo weight. This was crucial both in developing a liquid offload plan and in reviewing stability. Not only was the "found" cargo weight higher than the "lost" DFM but the overall cargo Center of Gravity was 12-ft higher than originally provided due to stowing vehicles on higher decks rather than lower in the holds. These revisions resulted in substantially less GM margin than anticipated.

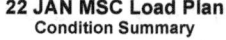

22 JAN MSC Load Plan
Condition Summary

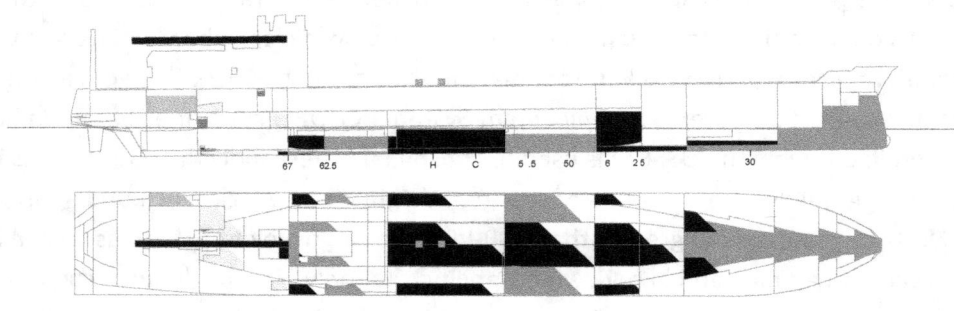

Group	Weight LT	VCG Ft-BL	LCG Ft-MS	TCG Ft-CL	FSt ft-LT
Lightship	26,539	41.35	54.97A	0.00	0
Diesel Oil	246	56.15	307.32A	44.97F	255
Lube Oil	56	30.18	268.63A	13.56F	188
Fresh Water	288	27.59	249.46A	2.72P	2,548
SW Ballast	3,767	15.42	173.65F	0.34P	26,170
CARGO/JP-5	489	15.65	71.29F	0.51S	70,274
DFM	2,428	12.20	32.88F	6.81S	13,779
Misc.	37	2.82	188.23A	0.04S	3,094
CREW, STORES	173	118.00	270.00A	0.00	0
Holds	0	--	--	--	0
Misc. Weights	244	72.47	41.36A	0.35P	0
In Hold	3,024	36.37	50.99F	0.78P	0
On Deck	5	85.08	127.56F	0.00	0
Displacement	37,296	36.59	20.41A	0.01S	116,307
Deadweight	10,757				
Avail Deadweight	14,248	--SUMMER--			

Stability			Trim		
KMt	46.04	ft	Specific Gravity	1.025	
VCG (Upright)	36.59	ft	LCF Draft	25.23	ft
GMt (Solid)	9.44	ft	LCF	11.76A	Ft-MS
FS Correction	3.12	ft	LCB	5.36A	Ft-MS
GMt (Corrected)	6.33	ft	LCG	20.41A	Ft-MS
GMt Required	5.01	ft	TP1in	138.7	LT/in
GMt Margin	1.31	ft	MT1in	5,261	ft-LT/in
--Req GM--			Trim at Perps	8.90A	ft
			Heel Angle	0.12S	deg
			Propeller Immersion	126.47	%
Drafts - Perps			**Drafts - Marks**		
AP	29.54 (29-6.5	ft	Aft	29.12 (29-1.4	ft
MS	25.09 (25-1.1	ft	MS	25.14 (25-1.6	ft
FP	20.64 (20-7.7	ft	Fwd	20.71 (20-8.6	ft
Strength --At Sea--					
Shear (Min)	-2,752	LT	153.50F Ft-MS	--	%
Shear (Max)	3,480	LT	193.00A Ft-MS	96.87	%
Shear (Max %Allow)	3,480	LT	193.00A Ft-MS	96.87	%
Moment (Max Hog)	856,583H	ft-LT	60.08A Ft-MS	--	%
Moment (Max %Allow)	630,710H	ft-LT	193.00A Ft-MS	31.08	%
Notes					
Drafts from Keel					
Hull from Tables					
Tanks from Tables					

Figure 10: Provided Departure Condition

31 JAN Updated Cargo & Ballast Departure
Condition Summary

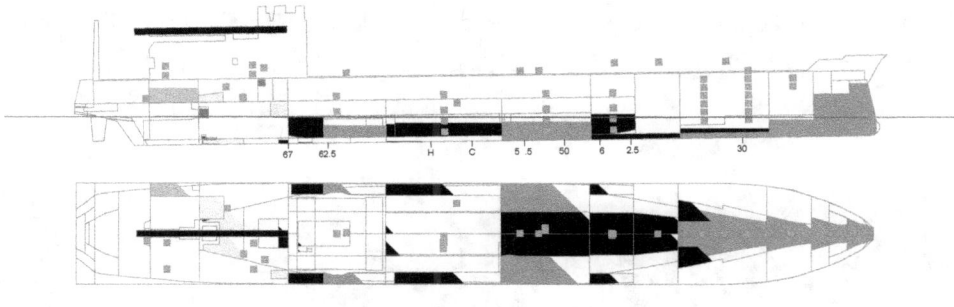

Group	Weight LT	VCG Ft-BL	LCG Ft-MS	TCG Ft-CL	FSt ft-LT
Lightship	26,539	41.35	54.97A	0.00	0
Diesel Oil	218	56.15	307.32A	44.97F	255
Lube Oil	60	32.02	285.87A	12.81F	177
Fresh Water	288	27.59	249.46A	2.72P	2,548
SW Ballast	3,462	16.31	189.03F	0.61P	16,482
CARGO/JP-5	625	16.46	18.04F	0.67S	70,003
DFM	2,022	11.33	53.76F	1.68S	12,311
Misc.	37	2.82	188.23A	0.04S	3,094
CREW, STORES	173	118.00	270.00A	0.00	0
Holds	0	--	--	--	0
Misc. Weights	3,817	48.99	0.52A	2.24S	0
In Hold	0	--	--	--	0
On Deck	0	--	--	--	0
Displacement	37,241	38.04	24.02A	0.03P	104,869
Deadweight	10,702				
Avail Deadweight	14,303	--SUMMER--			

Stability			Trim	
KMt	46.06	ft	Specific Gravity	1.025
VCG (Upright)	38.04	ft	LCF Draft	25.19 ft
GMt (Solid)	8.01	ft	LCF	11.74A Ft-MS
FS Correction	2.82	ft	LCB	5.35A Ft-MS
GMt (Corrected)	5.20	ft	LCG	24.02A Ft-MS
GMt Required	5.03	ft	TP1in	138.7 LT/in
GMt Margin	0.17	ft	MT1in	5,258 ft-LT/in
--Req GM--			Trim at Perps	11.02A ft
			Heel Angle	0.33P deg
			Propeller Immersion	130.72 %
Drafts - Perps			**Drafts - Marks**	
AP	30.54 (30-6.4	ft	Aft	30.02 (30-0.2 ft
MS	25.03 (25-0.3	ft	MS	25.08 (25-1.0 ft
FP	19.51 (19-6.2	ft	Fwd	19.60 (19-7.2 ft
Strength --At Sea--				
Shear (Min)	-2,938	LT	153.50F Ft-MS	74.54 %
Shear (Max)	3,840	LT	193.00A Ft-MS	106.88 %
Shear (Max %Allow)	3,840	LT	193.00A Ft-MS	106.88 %
Moment (Max Hog)	931,309H	ft-LT	57.98A Ft-MS	-- %
Moment (Max %Allow)	785,184H	ft-LT	152.50A Ft-MS	33.27 %
Notes				
Drafts from Keel				
Hull from Tables				
Tanks from Tables				

Figure 11: Actual Departure Condition

GROUNDING

As an initial dive survey had been performed within 48 hours of the grounding the location of grounding points was well known early in the salvage. The ground was modeled in POSSE as a bed of pinnacles representing the coral shelf beneath Holds #3A and 4 and two individual pinnacles representing the smaller ground point farther aft on the starboard side.

Figure 12: Ground Definition

The default pinnacle definitions provided an accurate representation of the KOCAK at the observed starboard drafts and heel taken during a mid-tide survey. However, initially POSSE predicted KOCAK's heel would vary by over 2 degrees through the tide cycle while it was known that she maintained a constant 1.5 degree port list. To correct this the spring constants on the port side pinnacles were stiffened while those on the starboard side were reduced. After a number of iterations a set of pinnacles were defined that maintained KOCAK at 1.5 degrees throughout the tide cycle. This grounding model proved accurate through all weight shift, lightering, and refloating operations.

31 JAN 1434 (Current Loads)
Grounding Summary

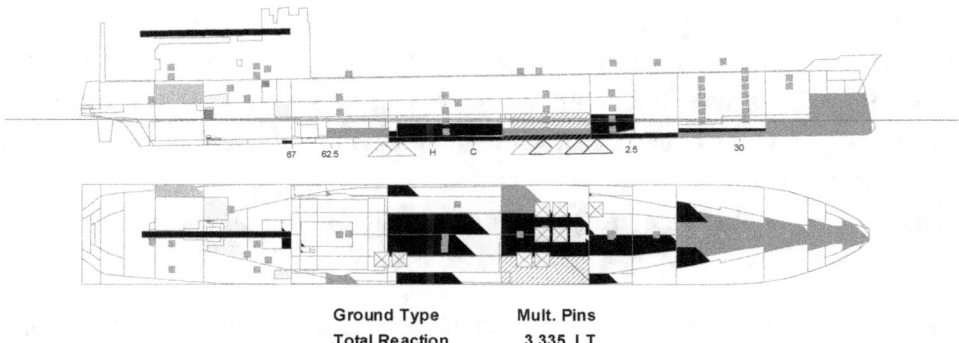

Ground Type	Mult. Pins
Total Reaction	3,335 LT
LCR	0.03A Ft-MS
TCR	8.69S Ft-BL
Force to Free	5,002 LT
Eff. Friction Coeff.	1.50
Tide Height	4.49 ft

Pinnacle Details		1	2	3	4	5	6	7
		Shelf 1-3	Shelf 2-3	Shelf 9-3	Shelf 10-1	Shelf 10-2	Shelf 10-3	Shelf 11-1
Water Depth	ft	22.78	22.49	20.49	21.71	20.96	20.21	21.43
Hull Contact LCR	Ft-MS	100.00A	81.67A	46 67F	65 00F	65.00F	65.00F	83.33F
Hull Contact TCR	Ft-CL	26.38S	26.38S	26 38S	26 38P	0.00	26.38S	26.38P
Hull Contact VCR	Ft-BL	0.00	0.00	0 00	0 00	0.00	0.00	0.00
Hull Dist to Pin	ft	0.71	0.66	0 36	0.16	0.24	0.32	0.13
Ground Type		Rock	Rock	Rock	Rock	Rock	Rock	Rock
Coef of Friction		1.5	1.5	1.5	1.5	1.5	1 5	1 5
Spring Type		Parabolic	Parabolic	Parabolic	Parabolic	Parabolic	Parabolic	Parabolic
Spring Const		15.00	15.00	25 00	125 00	25.00	12.70	125.00
Spring Const Units		LT/in^2	LT/in^2	LT/in^2	LT/in^2	LT/in^2	LT/in^2	LT/in^2
Reaction	LT	774	689	390	443	184	160	273
Pin Compression	in	1.3	1.2	0.4	0.1	0.2	0 3	0.1

Pinnacle Details		8	9	10	11
		Shelf 11-2	Shelf 12-1	Shelf 12-2	Shelf 13-1
Water Depth	ft	20 68	21.15	20.40	20.88
Hull Contact LCR	Ft-MS	83 33F	101 67F	101.67F	120.00F
Hull Contact TCR	Ft-CL	0.00	26 38P	0.00	26.38P
Hull Contact VCR	Ft-BL	0 00	0 00	0.00	0.00
Hull Dist to Pin	ft	0 20	0 09	0.17	0.06
Ground Type		Rock	Rock	Rock	Rock
Coef of Friction		1.5	1.5	1.5	1 5
Spring Type		Parabolic	Parabolic	Parabolic	Parabolic
Spring Const		25 00	125 00	25.00	125.00
Spring Const Units		LT/in^2	LT/in^2	LT/in^2	LT/in^2
Reaction	LT	133	144	91	54
Pin Compression	in	0.1	0.0	0.1	0 0

Figure 13: Pinnacle Details

REFLOAT PLAN

PREVIOUS ACTIONS AND ASSUMPTIONS

Flooding into Hold 3A and through the dislodged watertight doors into 4 and 4A was controlled and all three holds dewatered. The slowed but continued ingress of water in Hold 3A was controlled through periodic pumping to a slop barge alongside. The intent and assumption for planning was that those spaces would remain dewatered throughout the refloat. Substantial pumping capacity remained staged in all three holds and could be activated to dewater spaces either internally within KOCAK or overboard if necessary.

To limit risk to the environment, DFM from Inboard Double Bottom Tanks #3P/S (above the coral shelf and in proximity to the damage in Hold 3A) was transferred aft to Inboard Double Bottom Tanks #4A P/S. 200 LT of Cargo Potable Water was also offloaded from Wing Tanks #5A P/S.

LIGHTERING PLAN

MSC tasked the small tanker SLNC PAX to receive fuel from the KOCAK. The Nippon Salvage barge MISHIMA was used as a breasting barge between KOCAK and PAX to keep PAX in the deep water to port of KOCAK.

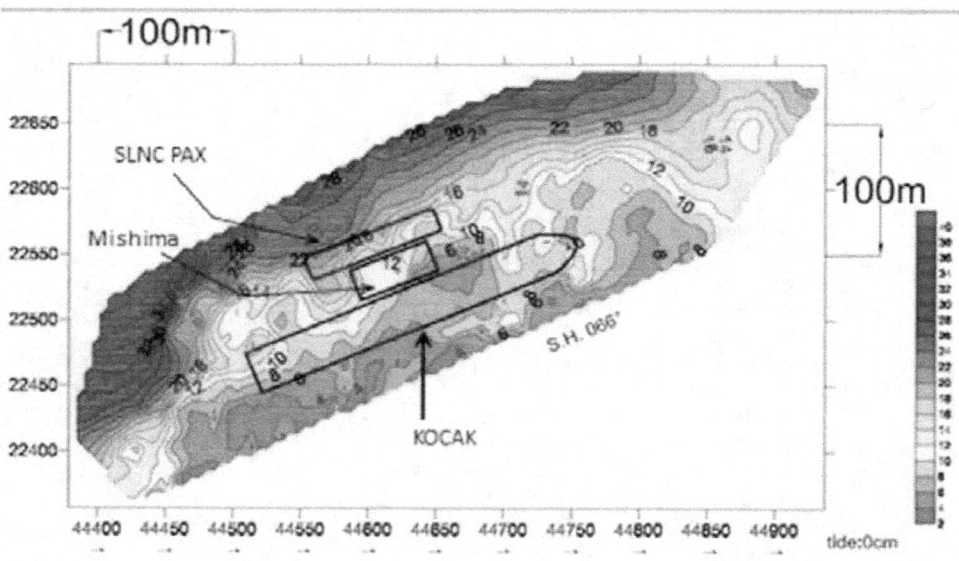

Figure 14: Lightering Arrangement

The selection of DFM tanks to be lightered was made with considerations towards regaining buoyancy, preserving stability, and limiting the risk to the environment. Approximately 9,000 bbl of DFM was to be offloaded from Wing Tanks #3 P/S, Inboard Double Bottom Tanks #4 P/S, and Inboard Double Bottom Tanks #4A P/S. This would retain approximately 100 bbl in each of the offloaded tanks to account for fuel that could not be reached from the primary pumps and the desire not to expend time with lengthy

14

stripping operations. KOCAK's Fuel Oil transfer system is rated at 1000 bbl/hr therefore the total transfer was estimated to take approximately 10 hours and complete during daylight. KOCAK carried two grades of DFM: F76 and MGO. The intent was to segregate the two fuels into separate tanks on PAX to facilitate reuse.

Comp	Mat'l	Vol (bbl)	Vol (gal)
WING TNK #3S	F76	1112	46704
DBTK#4P INBD	F76	1573	66066
DBTK#4S INBD	F76	1662	69804
DBTK#4AP INB	MGO	2427	101934
DBTK#4AS INB	MGO	2427	101934

Figure 15: Fuel Lightering

DFM was to be retained in the Diesel Oil Storage tanks for ship's service and propulsion. DFM was also to be retained in Inboard Wing Tanks #4A P/S for stability and trim. There was no indication of damage to these tanks and they are protected from damage by the double bottom. Additionally, ballast water was to be added to the Outboard Double Bottom Tanks #5 P/S to ensure a minimum ground reaction of 1000 LT to keep KOCAK stable through the next high tide prior to refloat. Fuel Oil removal operations were scheduled to complete the day prior to refloat in order to give time for the fuel tanker to be disconnected and removed as well as preparations made for final deballasting for refloat.

DEBALLASTING AND REFLOAT PLAN

Deballasting would commence with appropriate time to complete pumping operations prior to high tide. Ballast water was to be removed from the Outboard Double Bottom Tanks #5 P/S, and the Forepeak Tank. This would raise the bow of KOCAK enough to float off the coral shelf beneath Hold 4 at high tide and clear the shelf by 6 inches but also provide the maximum available parallel rise to maintain the aft draft at sailing level and prevent the rudder and propeller from impacting the reef during extraction. The last ballast move was to offload water from the #5 Wing Tank Stbd and ballasting into the #5 Wing Tank Port thus increasing the port list to facilitate rolling off the coral pinnacle on the starboard side.

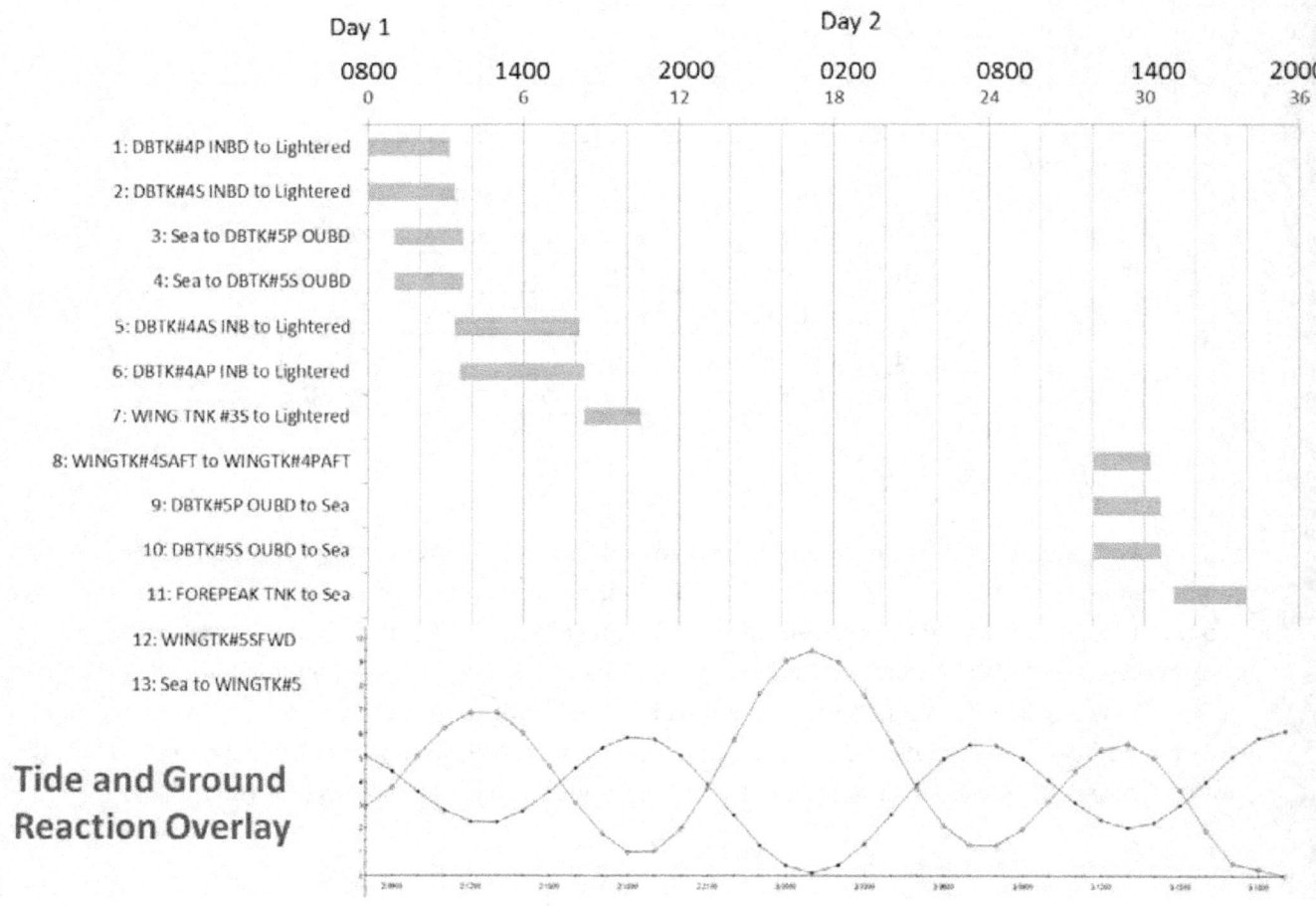

Figure 16: Lightering and Refloat Timeline

STABILTY

At refloat KOCAK would not meet the required GM from her Trim and Stability Book. However, that curve is based upon passing the worst case scenario of her one-compartment damaged stability requirement. As uncontrollable flooding into main spaces was not considered to be likely during the refloat, her afloat stability was compared to the intact requirements of the US Navy, US Coast Guard, and International Maritime Organization. Even with the known compromised spaces KOCAK still passed intact stability requirements.

Aflt
Righting Arm Summary

Angle deg	GZ ft	Draft AP ft	Draft FP ft	Trim deg	Flooded LT	CDisp LT	CTrim ft	Iter	#Calcs
0.00	-0.19	30.90	16.16	1.10A	1,396	0	0 00	5	5
1 00P	-0.10	30.90	16.15	1.10A	1,400	0	0 00	2	2
1 97P	0.00	30.89	16.16	1.10A	1,403	0	0 00	2	2
5 00P	0.32	30.82	16.19	1.09A	1,415	0	0 01	2	2
10 00P	1.02	30.54	16.17	1.07A	1,370	0	0 00	3	3
20 00P	3.12	29.05	16.26	0.96A	1,199	0	0 00	3	3
30 00P	5.22	26.31	15.84	0.78A	1,006	0	0 00	4	4
45 00P	7.47	17.86	12.05	0.43A	909	0	0 01	6	6
60 00P	7.58	1.85	0.72	0.08A	909	0	0 00	8	8
75 00P	4.10	-40.71	-34.40	0.47F	909	0	0 00	10	10
								45	45

Notes

GZ Curve from Offsets

Tanks from Offsets

Disp. of Remaining Intact Hull = 33,842

GZ Area Summation

PASS	GZ Area Summation		Value	Required
PASS	Area to 30.00	ft-deg	65.90	>=10.34
PASS	Area to 40.00	ft-deg	126.83	>=16.92
PASS	Area 30.00 to 40.00	ft-deg	60.93	>=5.64
PASS	Angle at Maximum GZ	deg	53.54	>=25.00
PASS	Maximum GZ Above 30 Deg	ft	7.95	>=0.66
PASS	Initial Metacentric Height	ft	5.63	>=0.49

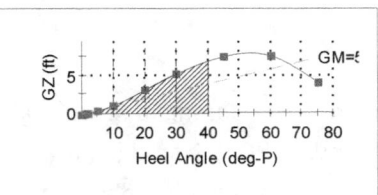

USCG Weather Criteria

PASS	USCG Weather		Value	Required
PASS	Min GMt	ft	5.63	>=0.06

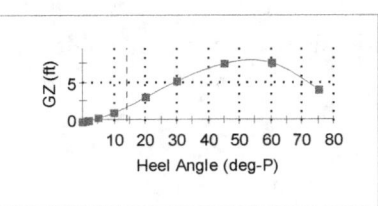

U.S. Navy DDS079-1: Beam Wind and Rolling Custom

PASS	U.S. Navy DDS079-1: Beam Wind and Rolling Custom		Value	Required
PASS	Wind Heel	deg	9.99	<=25.00
PASS	Maximum Righting Arm		0.13	<=0.60
PASS	Area 1	ft-deg	330.19	>=54.90

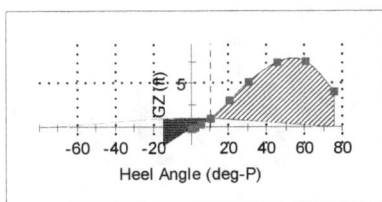

17

2008 IS Code 2.2 General Criteria

PASS	2008 IS Code 2.2 General Criteria		Value	Required
PASS	Area to 30.00	ft-deg	65.90	>=10.34
PASS	Area to 40.00	ft-deg	126.83	>=16.92
PASS	Area 30.00 to 40.00	ft-deg	60.93	>=5.64
--	Angle to Downflooding	deg	N/A	
PASS	Angle at Maximum GZ	deg	53.54	>=25.00
PASS	Maximum GZ Above 30 Deg	ft	7.95	>=0.66
PASS	Initial Metacentric Height	ft	5.63	>=0.49

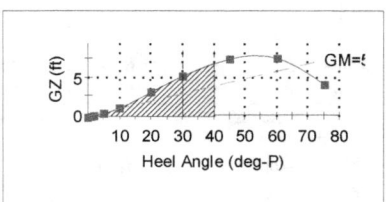

2008 IS Code 2.3 Weather Criteria

PASS	2008 IS Code 2.3 Weather Criteria		Value	Required
PASS	Heeling Angle at LW1	deg	4.47	<=16.00
PASS	Area Ratio B/A		9.23	>=1.00

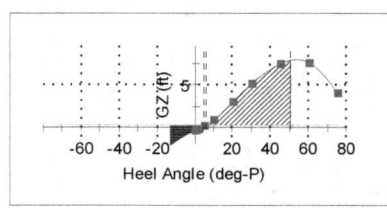

Figure 17: Intact GZ Criteria Summary

STRENGTH

Stresses applied to the damaged structural areas during refloating was considered a risk and required additional review. A POSSE .smd file at Frame 46 had been prepared as part of the initial POSSE model development and was considered an appropriate representation of the structure at the damaged Frame 45. For analysis, it was assumed that all structural members with proximity to the known damage were completely ineffective. This was an extremely conservative assumption as it was clear that many members had only been minimally deformed and would retain a substantial portion of their intact strength.

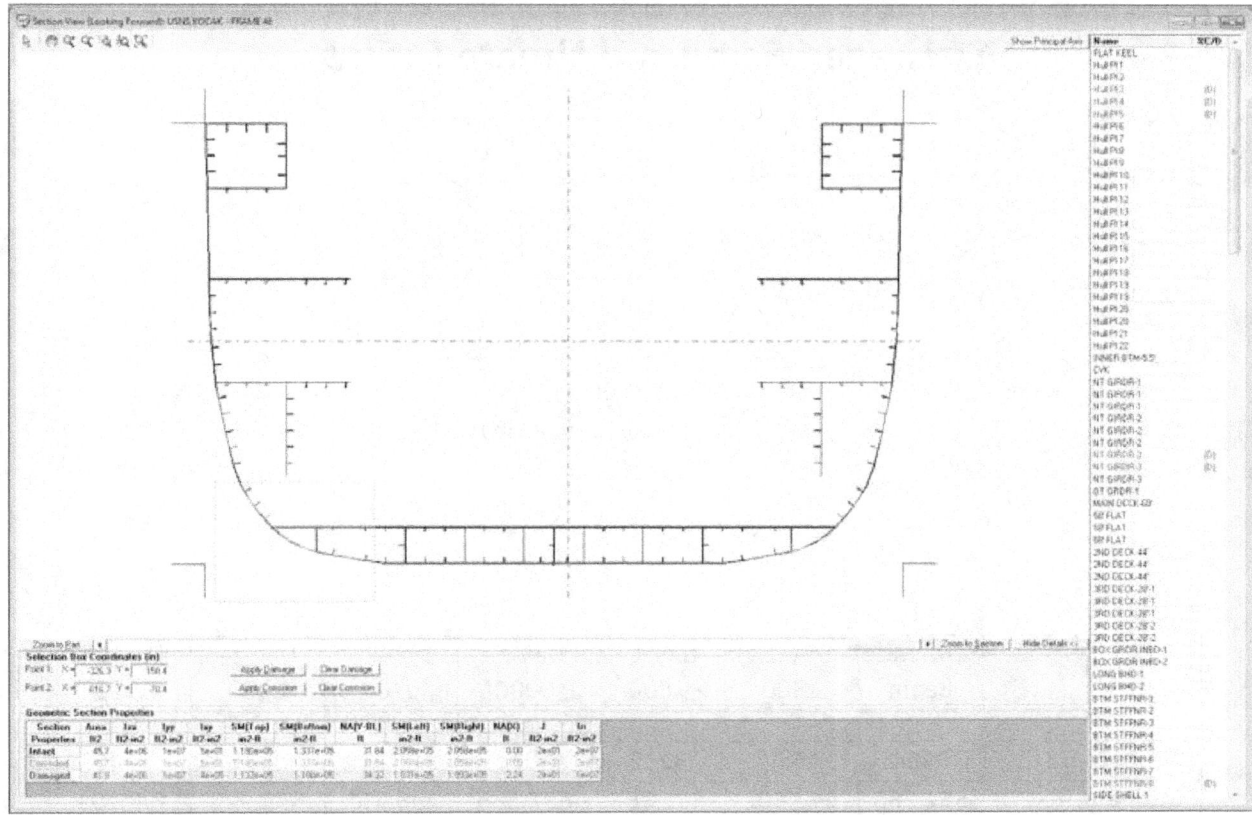

Figure 18: Assumed Structural Damage

An Ultimate Strength (ULTSTR) analysis was performed on both the intact and damaged sections. Initial failure of an individual structural member of the damaged section occurred at 1.2E6 ft-LT with cascading complete failure at 1.5E6 ft-LT. Bending stress at Frame 45 was kept below 0.7E6 ft-LT providing a Factor of Safety of approximately 2 or greater throughout the refloat.

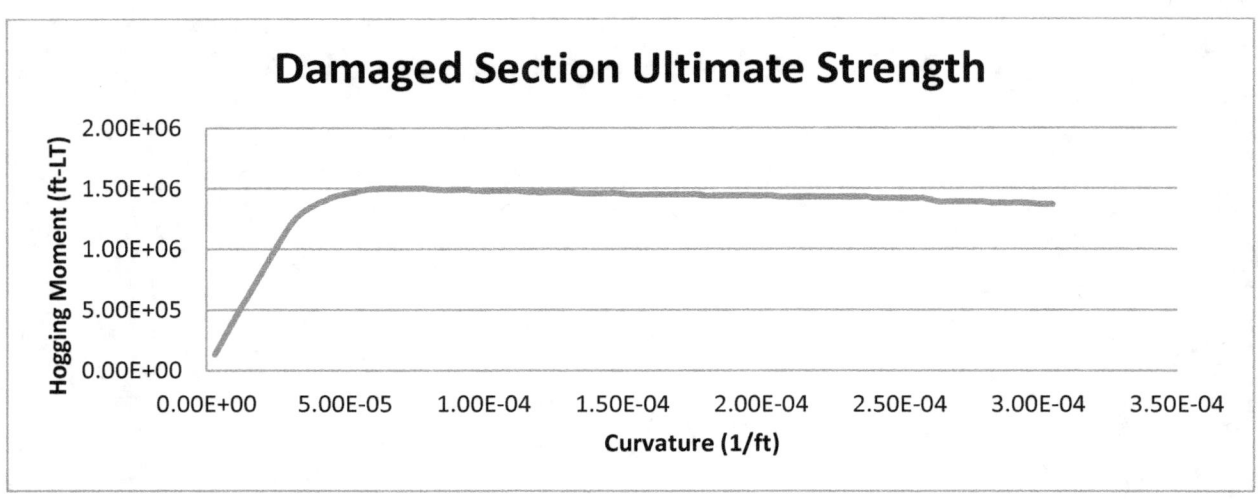

Figure 19: Damaged Section ULTSTR

	Offload Begin	Day 1 - 1300	Day 1 - 1800	Day 2 - 0000	Day 2 - 0700	Day 2 - 1300	Day 2 - 1900 Aflt
Shear (LT)	3384	4437	3292	5063	3324	4516	3146
Moment (ft-LT)	552,250	642,402	546,267	697,586	549,155	649,973	498,291
Keel Stress (ksi)	11.49	13.37	11.37	14.51	11.43	13.52	10.37
SF Intact	3.17	2.72	3.20	2.51	3.19	2.69	3.51
SF Initial Damaged	2.17	1.87	2.20	1.72	2.19	1.85	2.41
SF Complete Damaged	2.72	2.33	2.75	2.15	2.73	2.31	3.01

Figure 20: Refloat Bending Moment

CONTINGENCIES

Additional ballast was available for removal from the Forepeak and Deep Tank #1 if more trim was necessary. Also, fittings and gauges were rigged to the cross-connected damaged Ballast Tanks #4 Wing P/S to allow for compressed air dewatering of the tanks through the damaged bottom plating.

LIGHTERING AND REFLOAT OPERATIONS

LIGHTERING

Early on the morning of 2 February, 2015, M/T SLNC PAX came alongside the Nippon salvage barge MISHIMA which was already secure to the port side of KOCAK. After attaching mooring lines and transfer hoses Fuel Oil transfer from KOCAK to PAX commenced at 0942.

Figure 21: Lightering Operations

DFM transfer progressed significantly faster than anticipated. This combined with favorable weather throughout the lightering operation and forecast to continue through the next day provided an opportunity to offload more fuel than had been originally planned. After some debate an additional 1900 bbls (300 LT) of fuel was transferred out of KOCAK's #4 Wing Tanks P/S and the risk of reduced ground reaction at the high tide prior to refloat was accepted.

Comp	Mat'l	Planned Offload		Actual Offload	
		Vol (bbl)	Vol (gal)	Vol (bbl)	Vol (gal)
WING TNK #3S	F76	1112	46704	1,188	49896
DBTK#4P INBD	F76	1573	66066	1,528	64176
DBTK#4S INBD	F76	1662	69804	1,523	63966
DBTK#4AP INB	MGO	2427	101934	2,377	99834
DBTK#4AS INB	MGO	2427	101934	2,332	97944
WINGTK#4PAFT	MGO	0	0	636	26712
WINGTK#4SAFT	MGO	0	0	1,503	63126
TOTAL		9201	386442	11087	465654

Figure 22: Lightering Actuals

DEBALLASTING AND REFLOAT

Deballasting did not go as smoothly as lightering. The first step was to offload the ballast in Outboard Double Bottom Tanks #5 P/S that had been added the previous day to counter the weight lost during lightering. Those tanks are not often used and the pumps were unable to maintain suction for offload. At approximately 1400, the point at which the majority of deballasting was scheduled to be complete and list control tanks were to be prepared to assist refloating at the 1830 high tide, attempts to deballast the Outboard Double Bottom Tanks #5 P/S were halted and the refloat plan was adjusted to pump additional ballast water from the Forepeak and #1 Deep Tanks. Additionally, compressed air was applied to the #4 Wing Ballast Tanks P/S. The compressed air dewatering would partially supplant the parallel rise expected from the #5 Ballast tanks but the additional offload from the Forepeak and #1 Deep Tanks would increase trim risking impact of the propeller and rudder on the coral during extraction.

At approximately 1700 the combination of the rising tide and deballasting forward had resulted in noticeable movement of the bow as it floated off the forward coral shelf. The focus of pumping was then shifted to offloading the Wing Tank #5Fwd Stbd to heel off the starboard pinnacle. Concurrently, two tugs with a combined bollard pull of 100 MT began to periodically take strain on the stern. At 1730 KOCAK was pulled safely from the reef without damage to the propeller or rudder. After an internal damage survey to ensure the known flooding had not increased and no addition flooding was occurring the 2 degree list KOCAK had floated off with was corrected and she steamed under her own power to White Beach Naval Facility.

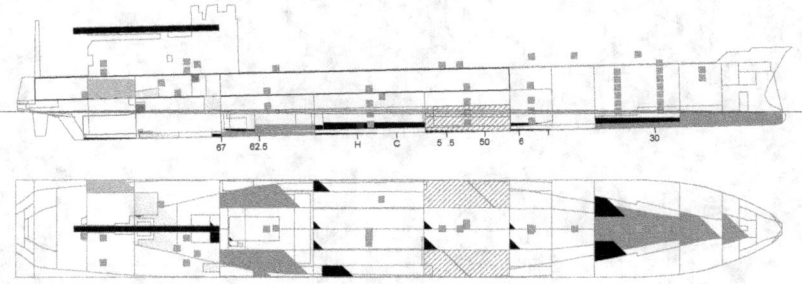

Loading

Displacement	34,611 LT	Specific Gravity	1.025
Deadweight	8,072 LT		

Stability		Trim	
GMt Upright (Corrected)	6.07 ft	LCF Draft	23 62 ft
GMt @ Equil	6.33 ft	LCF	23.73A Ft-MS
		LCB	37 31A Ft-MS
		LCG	36.72A Ft-MS
		KB	12.72 Ft-BL
		TCB	1 32P Ft-CL
		TCG	0 35P Ft-CL
		TP1in	138.1 LT/in
		MT1in	5,725 ft-LT/in
		Trim at Perps	17 22A ft
		Heel Angle	2.10P deg
		Propeller Immersion	135.66 %

Drafts - Perps		Drafts - Marks	
AP	31.70 (31-8.4) ft	Aft	30.89 (30-10.7) ft
MS	23.09 (23-1.1) ft	MS	23.18 (23-2.1) ft
FP	14.48 (14-5.8) ft	Fwd	14 61 (14-7.4) ft

Strength --At Sea--			
Shear (Min)	-3,364 LT	153.50F Ft-MS	85 35 %
Shear (Max)	3,907 LT	193.00A Ft-MS	108.76 %
Shear (Max %Allow)	3,907 LT	193.00A Ft-MS	108.76 %
Moment (Max Hog)	923,132H ft-LT	54.53A Ft-MS	--- %
Moment (Max %Allow)	787,124H ft-LT	152.50A Ft-MS	33 35 %

Notes

Drafts from Keel

Hull from Offsets

GMt from GZ Curve Slope

Tanks from Offsets

Figure 23: Refloat Condition

Figure 24: KOCAK Pierside

CONCLUSIONS/LESSONS LEARNED

The salvage of USNS SGT MATEJ KOCAK (T-AK 3005) was a successful operation which refloated the vessel on the first attempt without any fuel spilled or additional damage caused to either the ship or reef. This operation emphasized the advantages POSSE provides for complex salvage operations requiring all actions to balance considerations of ship stability, strength, external influences, and environmental concerns. A number of recent improvements to POSSE were utilized including:

- Observed drafts entry tool to calculate vessel attitude and ground reaction through available information including partial draft readings, heel/trim, freeboards, etc.
- Improved ground entry tools for multiple pinnacles.
- Detailed weight definitions to divide single weights into components.
- Multiple and modifiable GZ criteria.
- Individual file save and import options for tide cycles and lightering/weight transfer plans.

As with any operation there were also areas identified for improvement. The most significant area of potential improvement is a well-known concern during salvage operations. The loading information provided by the ship and the ship-owner did not fully reflect the as-loaded condition of the ship. A substantial amount of time was spent over the first few days of the operation confirming and correcting tank and cargo loads. Potential modifications to the POSSE software itself are fairly general and include:

24

- Improvements in the ability to define and determine the ground that accurately reflects the impact on the vessel throughout the tide cycle.
- File size: Plan files with a time sequence analysis would regularly exceed 50MB
- Program Speed: Operations within a large plan file, even ones that only impact one condition, would take an undesirably long time.

USNS MATEJ KOCAK
Emergent Repair Plan

Supervisor of Salvage (NAVSEA 00C)

13 February 2015

General Arrangements

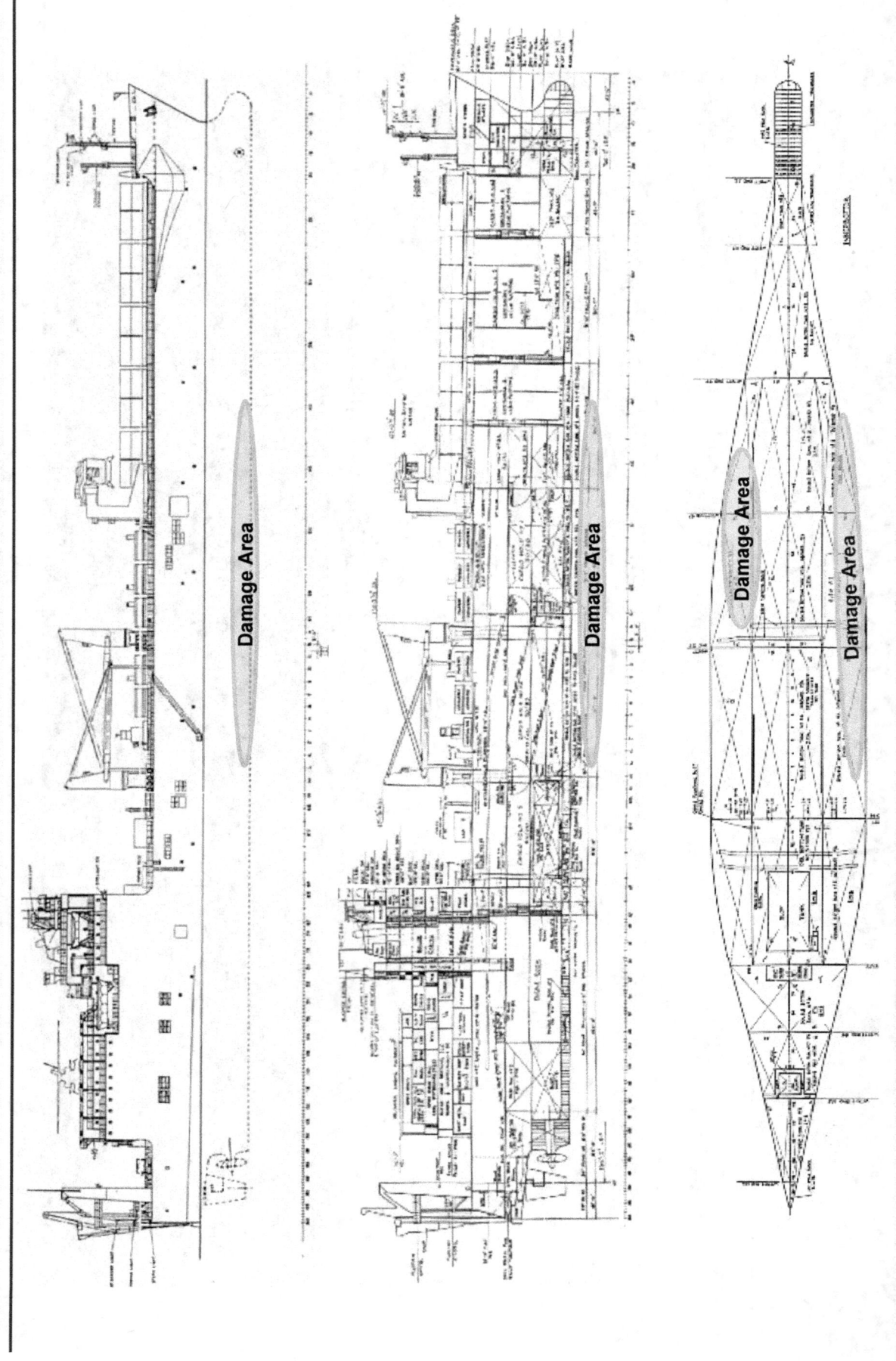

Overview: Shell to Double Bottom (D/B)

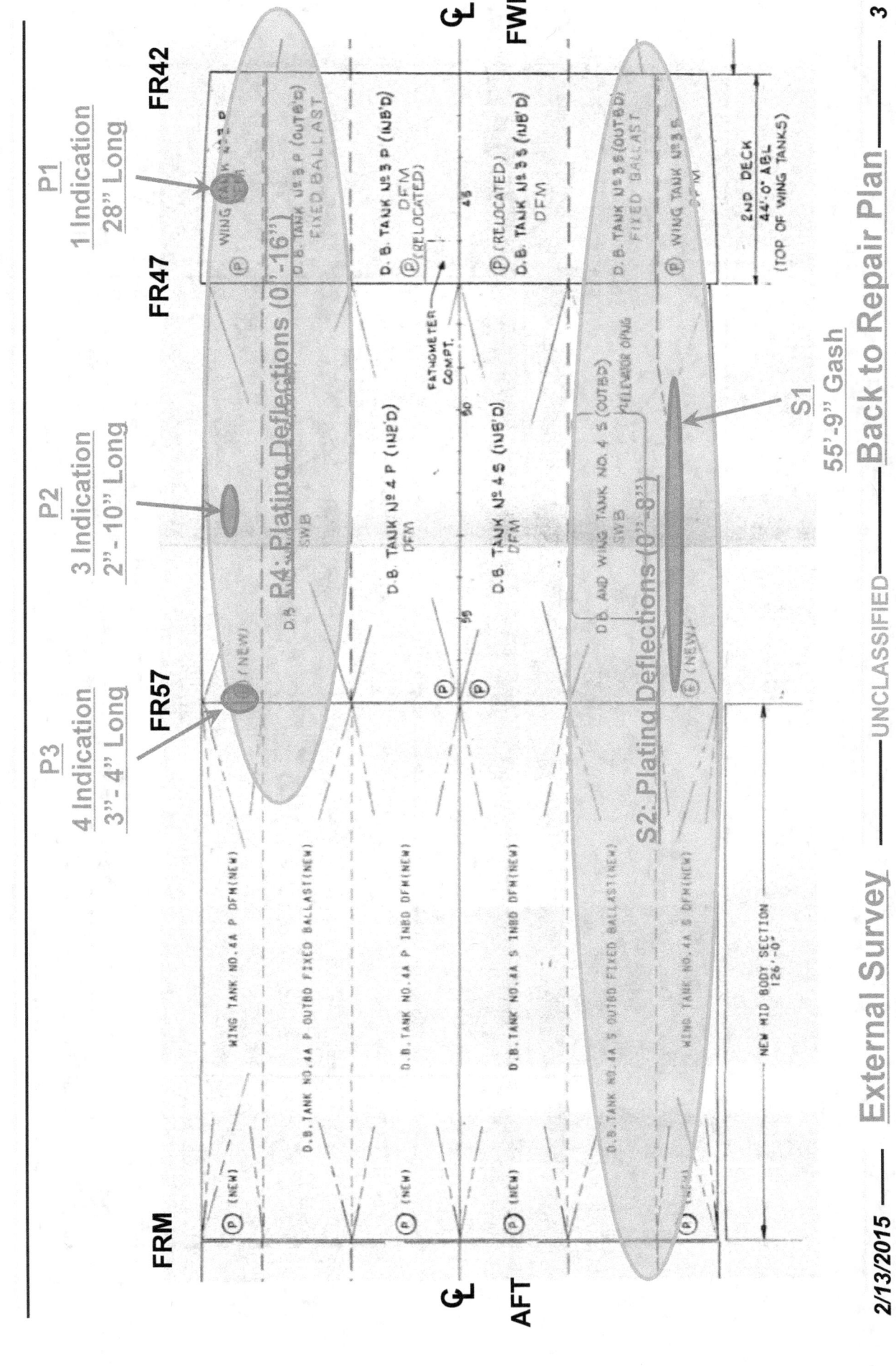

P1
1 Indication
28" Long

P2
3 Indication
2" – 10" Long

P3
4 Indication
3" – 4" Long

FR42

FR47

FR57

FRM

P4: Plating Deflections (0'–16")

S2: Plating Deflections (0" – 8")

S1

55'-9" Gash

Overview: D/B to Tank Top

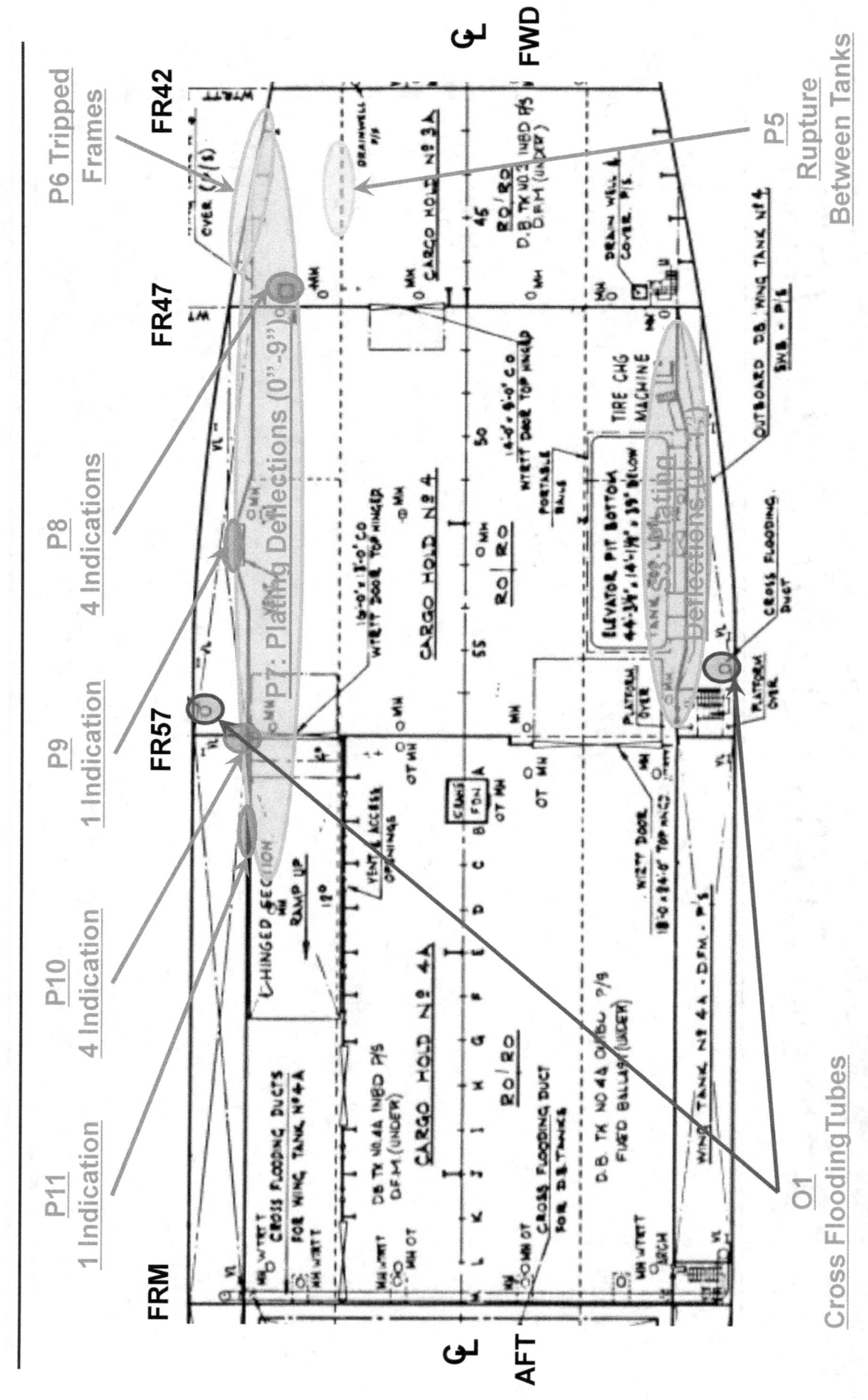

Overview: FR 47 WTB

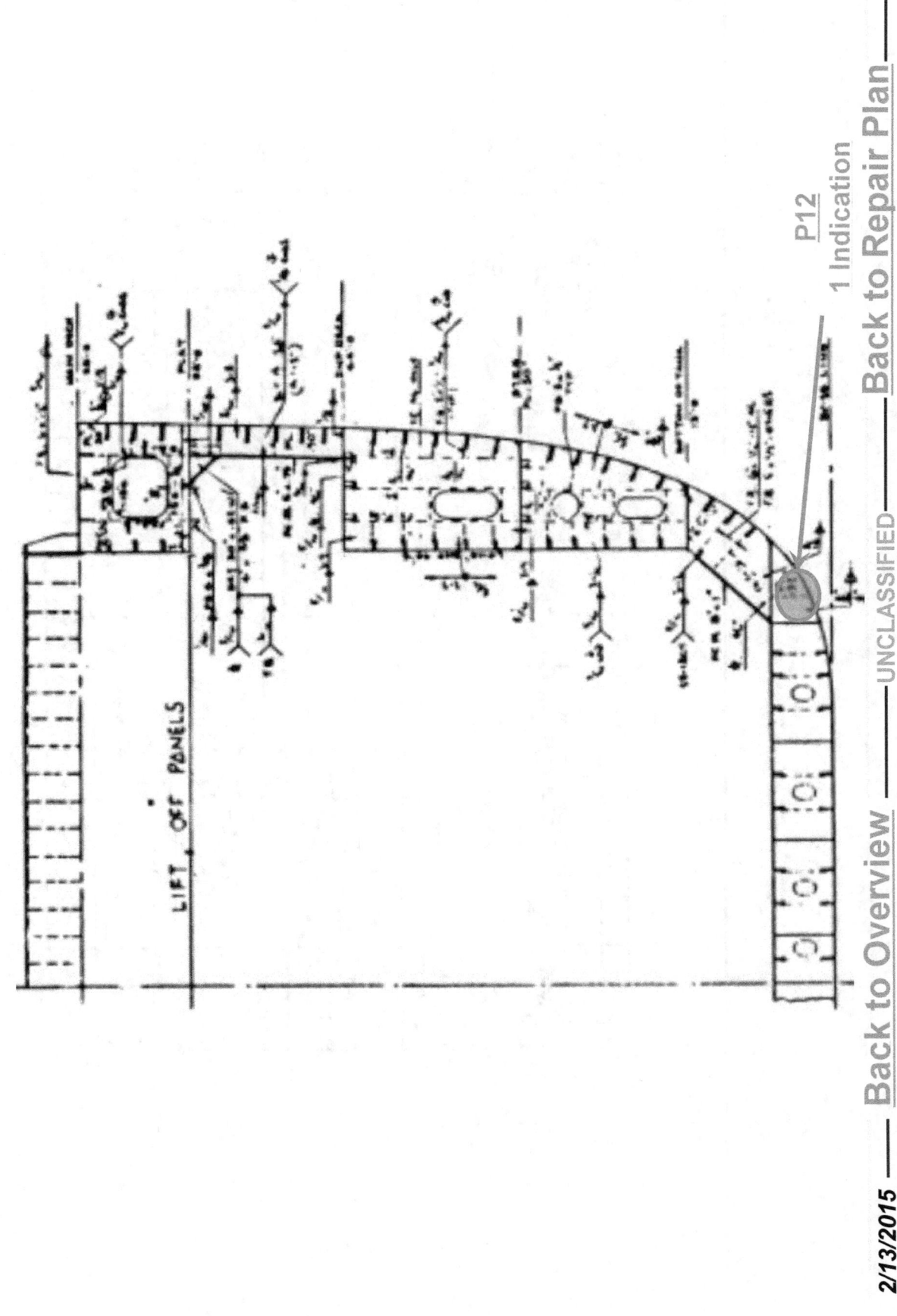

P12
1 Indication

Overview: FR 57 WTB

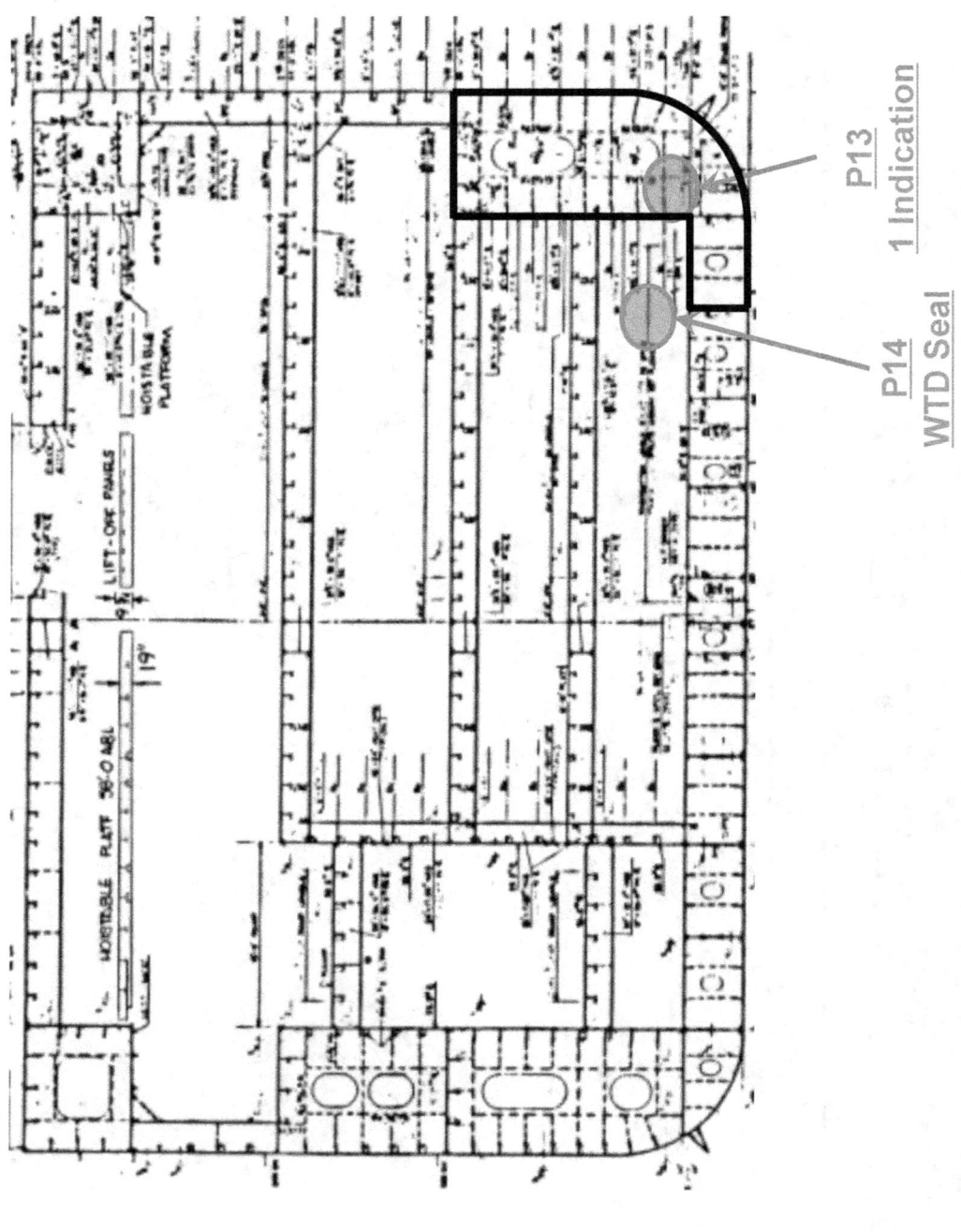

Repair Plan Summary

1. Restore Port Shell Plating with weld repair: P1, P2, P3 (PHX)

2. Arrest S1 crack propagation (PHX)

3. Isolate tanks 3A, 4 and 4A from the Cargo Holds: P8, P9, P10 and P11 with welding and epoxy repair (PHX).

4. Isolate 4A wing fuel tank from adjacent ballast tanks.

5. Isolate 4P D/B from 4S D/B, cross flooding tubes with mechanical blanking plates: (SMIT)

6. Restore cargo hold watertight integrity between holds 4 and 4A with door modification: P14 (PHX)

Departure Notes:

1. Repairs expected to be complete by 2/20

2. Departure condition for 4-P D/B tank (SWB) is filled to 5'

3. Departure condition for 4A-P wing tank (F/O) is empty.

Repair Plan Details

1. Restore Port Shell Plating: Weld Repairs (P1, P2, P3)

   a. Arrest/remove cracks (VT, MT, arc gouging, drill stop (min dia = 2X crack width).

   b. Port shell plate sealing (P1, P2, P3) with doubler plates (3 locations) and elliptical head patches as required to fit (min ¼" plate for doublers, 3/8" plate for elliptical heads).

   c. Underwater wet welding IAW ABS approved procedures

      1. austenitic (Ni) electrode for high C and CE (2 locations)

      2. mild steel electrode for low C and CE (3 locations).

2. Starboard Shell Crack Arresting - VT, MT, arc gouging (min dia = 2X crack width)

Repair Plan Details (cont'd)

3. Isolate Port tanks 3A, 4 and 4A from the Cargo Holds: P8, P9, P10 and P11

   a. Crack in 3A (FB) - weld repair tank top to cargo hold boundary.

   b. Crack in 4A (FO) – epoxy repair inside tank with shoring inside the tank to support.

   c. Cracks in 4 (SWB) - epoxy repair inside tank with shoring inside the tank to support.

4. Isolate 4A wing fuel tank from adjacent ballast tanks.

   a. epoxy repair inside tank with shoring inside the tank to support.

Repair Plan Details (cont'd)

5. Isolate 4P D/B from 4S D/B, cross flooding tubes with mechanical blanking plates: (SMIT)

   a. Mechanical Patches at cross connect tubes utilize 3/8" plate circular patch to cover 26" diameter tubes at upper end of each (port and stbd) tube. Circular patch is split to fit inside manhole and installed with 1-3/4" thick neoprene gasket. Gasket is compressed with turnbuckles jacking against the patch plate and the overhead of the cross connect tube box structure or strongbacks and j-Bolts. Flood water would put each patch and gasket in compression.

Repair Plan Details (cont'd)

6. Restore cargo hold watertight integrity between holds 4 and 4A with door modification (P14).

   a. Cut bottom of door to match tank top contour

   b. Replace existing shoe plate with ½" shoe plate

   c. Install door seal channel below the shoe plate

   d. Cut back the bottom 24" of the outboard side of the door to match the contour of the bent frame and modify side seal channel to match contour

   e. Secure closed door with turnbuckles to replace upper and lower door locks that were removed to facilitate door opening.

S1

Stbd, round bilge, into #4 O/B D/B wing tank (SWB): 55'-9" gash, 58" aft of FR50 to 38" fwd of 57, average 8" opening.

S2

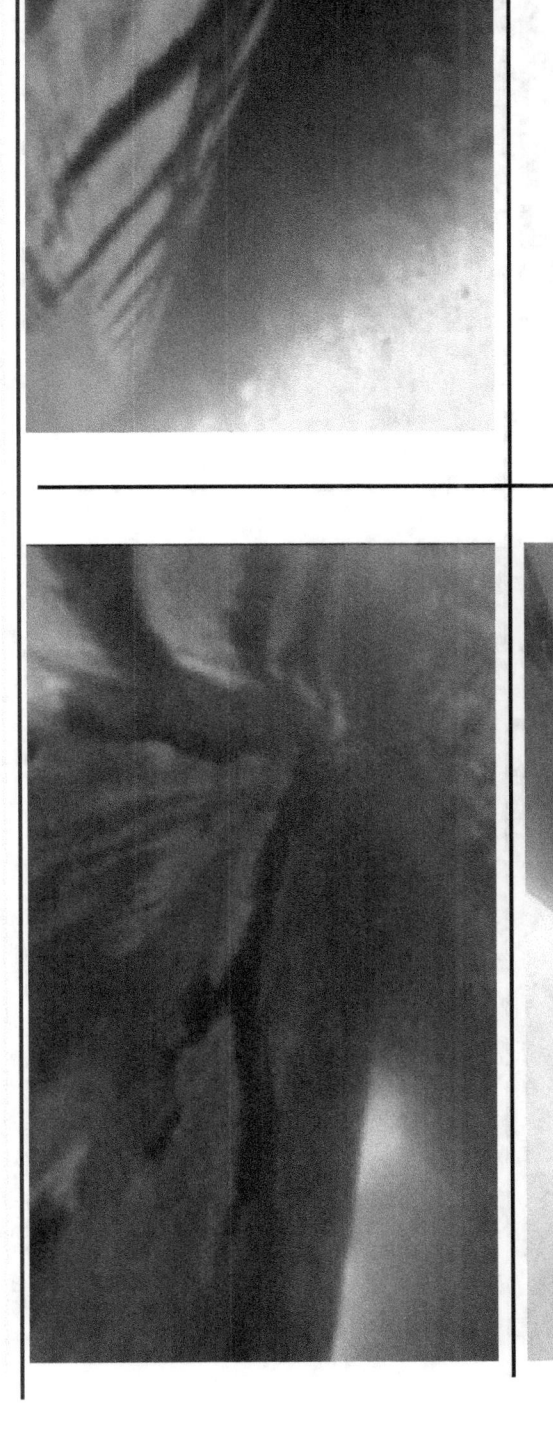

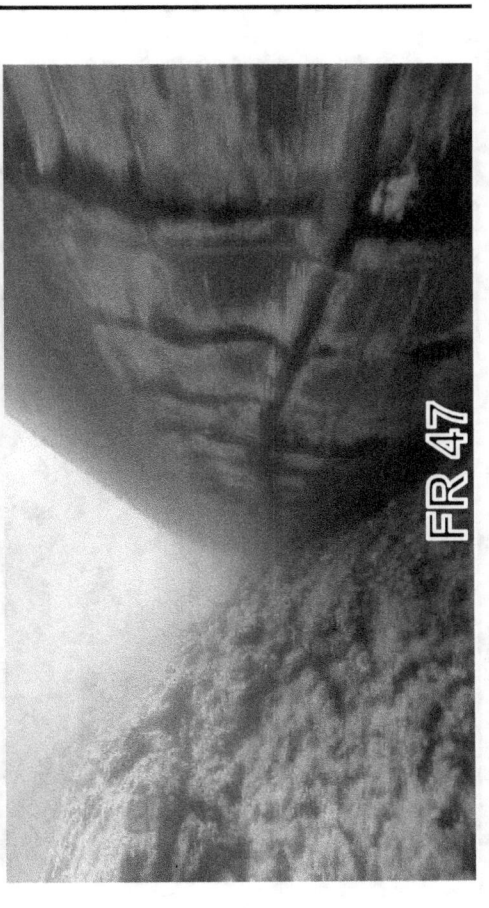

FR 47

Stbd, bilge keel and round bilge, FR42-FR62: plate deflection up to 8"

P1: Weld Repair (41" x 8" doubler)

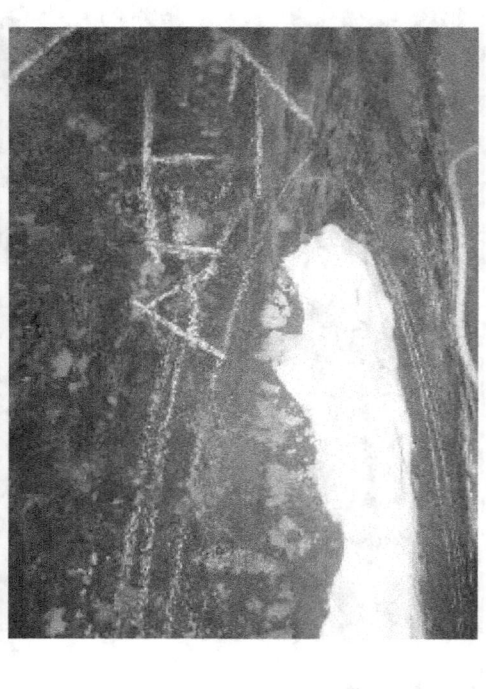

Port, round bilge, into #3 O/B D/B wing tank (FB): 28" indication, across FR 45 (PE-45)

P2: Weld Repair (12" dia elliptical head)

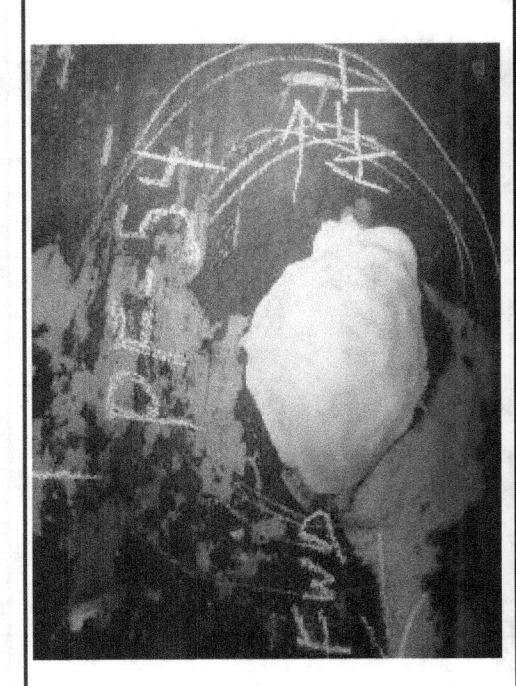

Port, round bilge, into #4 O/B D/B wing tank (SWB): 3 indications between FR52-54 (PF-54)

Back to Overview —— Back to Repair Plan

P3: Weld Repair (8" dia elliptical head, 10" x 4" doubler, 13" x 5" doubler)

Port, flat bottom, into #4 O/B D/B wing tank (SWB): 3 indications between FR56-57, ~31' from CL, up to 3" in length. Port, round bilge, into #4A O/B D/B wing tank (FB): 1 indication on FRA, 4" in length (PD-57I, PD-57 and PD-56)

P4 (no shell breach, crack arrest only)

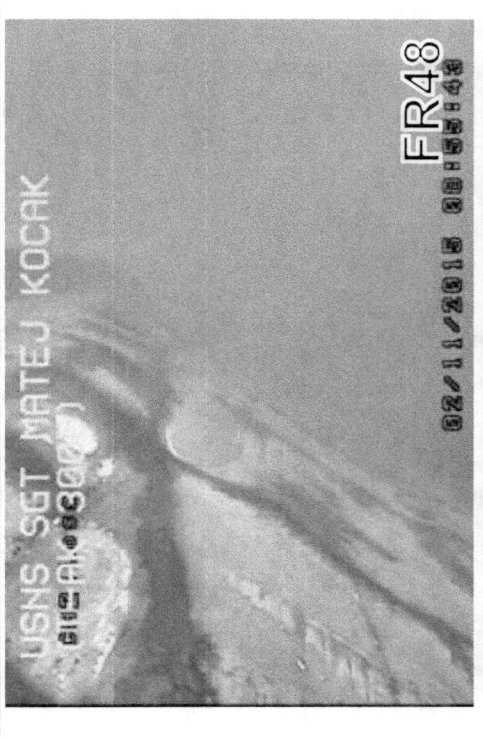

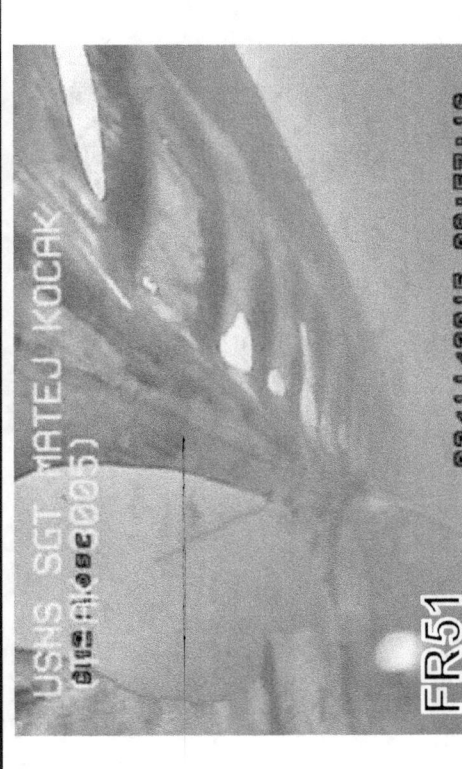

Port, bilge keel and shell plating, FR39-FRA: plate deflection up to 16"

Other: Port, bilge keel, between doubler and side shell: 1 indication 16" aft of FR 57, 32" long

P6

Transverse frames 44, 45, and 46 that have partially buckled between the decking and the longitudinal at the bottom of #3 O/B wing tank.

Back to Overview ———— UNCLASSIFIED ———— Back to Repair Plan

P7

Tank top decking deflected upwards, 0"-9", between FR43 and FRC.

P8: Weld Repair

#3 O/B D/B (FB) leak into #3A tank top deck: 4 locations where the fillet welds between the decking and the WTB have failed.

P9: Epoxy Repair

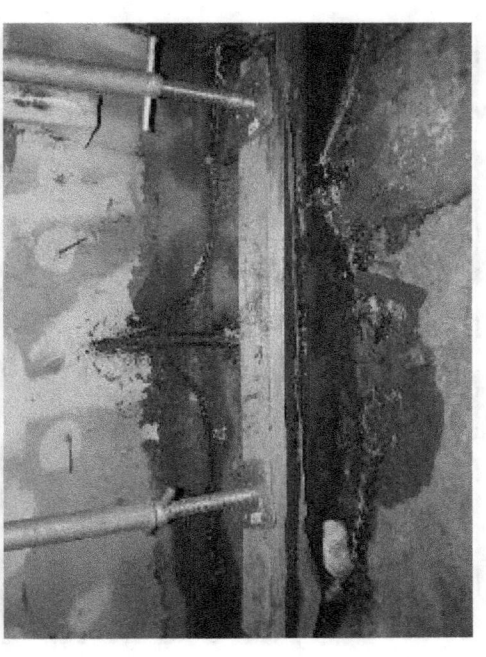

#4 O/B D/B (SWB) leak into 4 tank top deck: 48" long indication.

P10: Epoxy Repair

. #4 & #4A O/B D/B (SWB/FB) leak into tank top deck: 4 indications around WTD foundation. Location is patched and shored. No leaks when #4 O/B D/B tank is below tank top (5'-6" ABL), leak rate of less than 1 GPM when full.

P11: Epoxy Repair

#4A O/B D/B (F/O - Empty) leak into 4 tank top deck: 48" long indication. Patch will remain in place.

P12: Epoxy Repair

FR47, TT, 4-P D/B O/B

FR48 (looking forward)

Port side. WTB between #3 O/B D/B (FB) and #4 O/B D/B (SWB). Leaks at P4 stopped when #4 O/B D/B was dewatered.

P13: Soft Patch

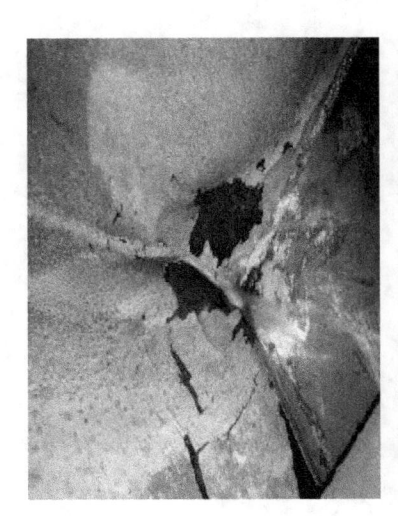

Port side WTB, between #4 O/B D/B (FB) and #4A O/B wing (DFM). Cracked fillet weld.

P14: Weld Repair

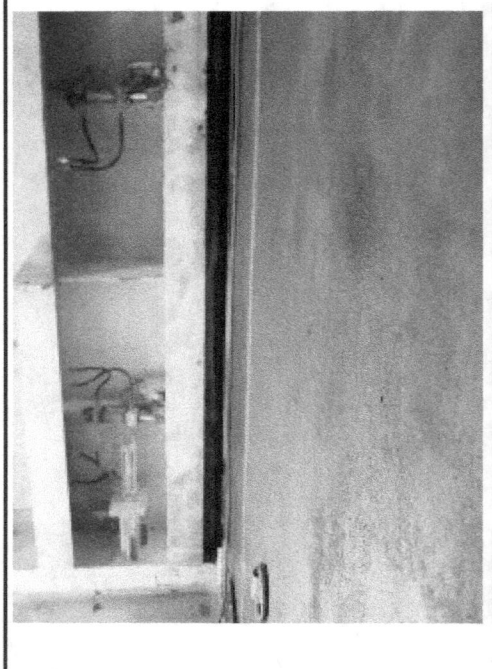

Port side WTD, floor deflections leave gap between door and floor and vertical sealing surfaces.

O1: Blank X-Flood Tubes

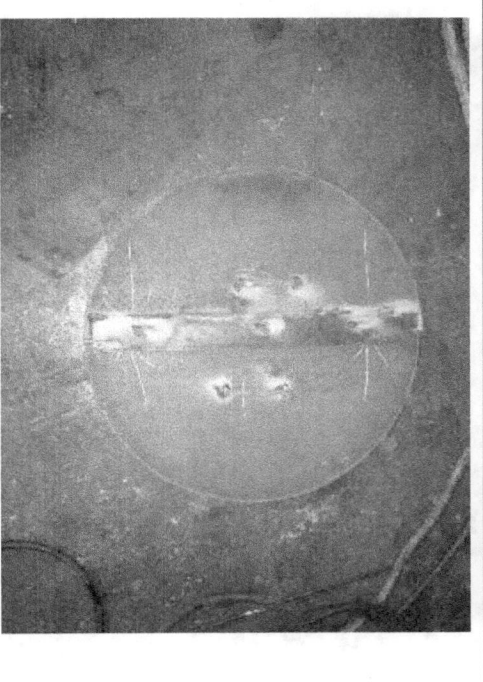 

 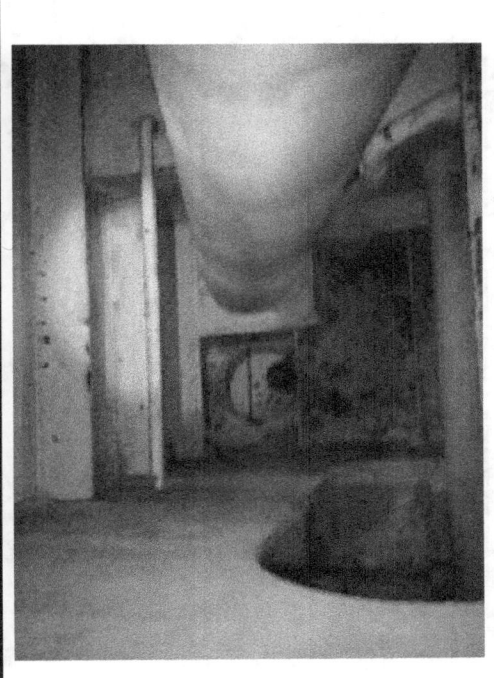

Blank cross flooding tubes in order to isolate 4-P O/B D/B tank from 4-S O/B D/B tank.

External Hull Survey: Stbd F47-F57

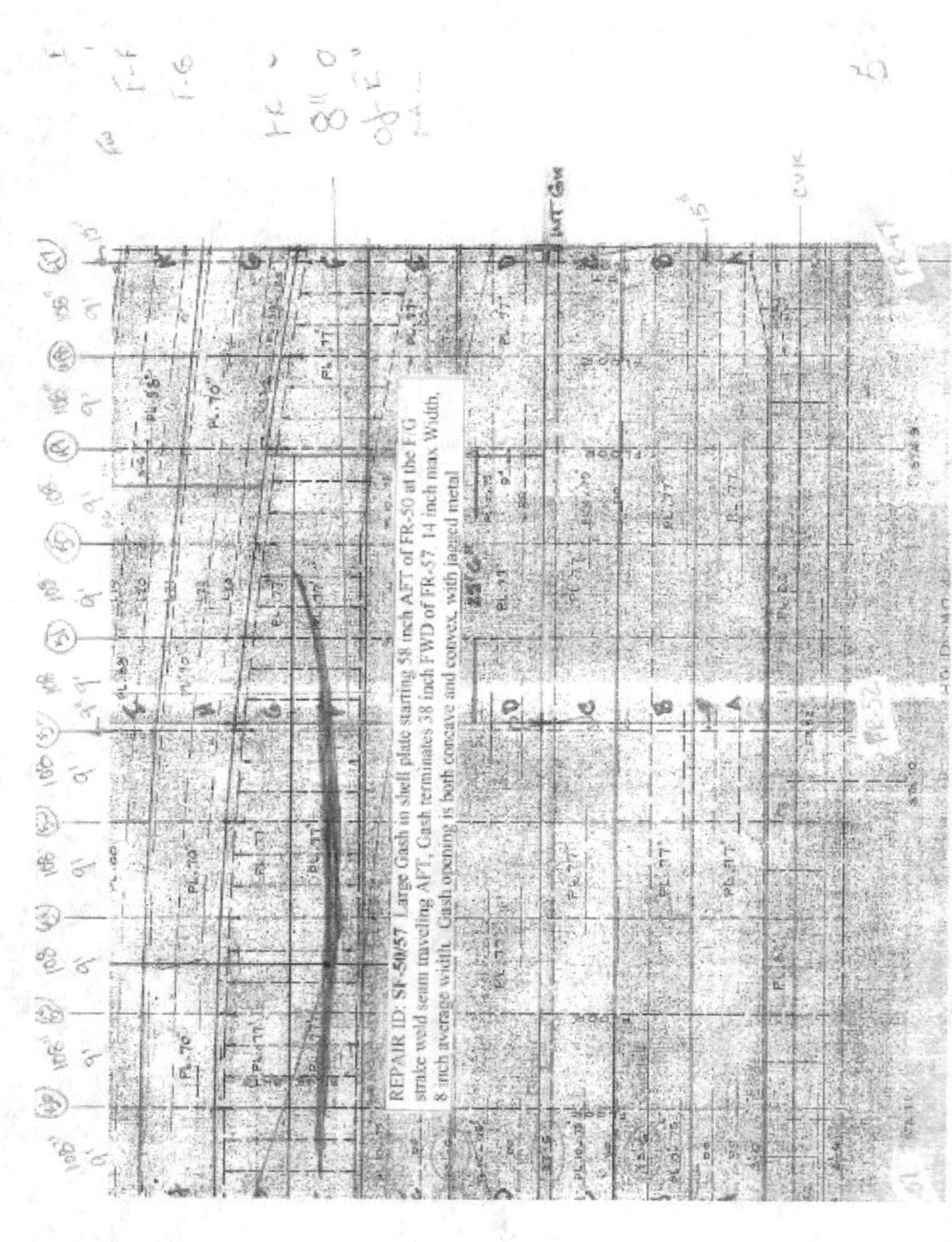

REPAIR ID: SF-50/57 Large Gash in shell plate starting 58 inch AFT of FR-50 at the F/G strake weld seam traveling AFT. Gash terminates 38 inch FWD of FR-57. 14 inch max. Width, 8 inch average width. Gash opening is both concave and convex, with jagged metal

External Hull Survey: Port F37-F47

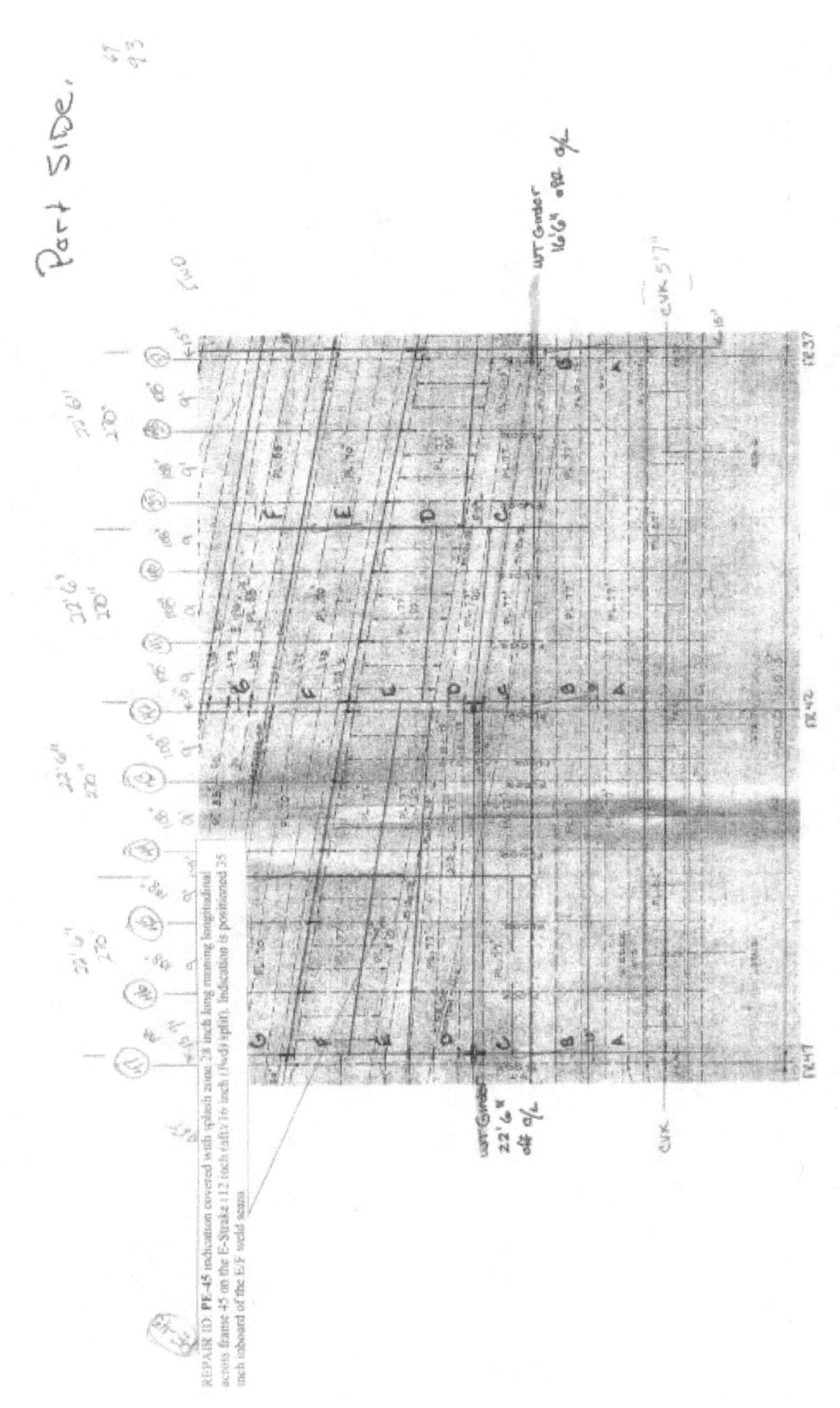

Port Side.

REPAIR ID: PF-45 indication covered with splash zone 24 inch long running longitudinal across frame 45 on the E-Strake (12 inch tall)(16 inch spring). Indication is positioned 35 inch inboard of the E-F weld seam

External Hull Survey: Port F47-F57

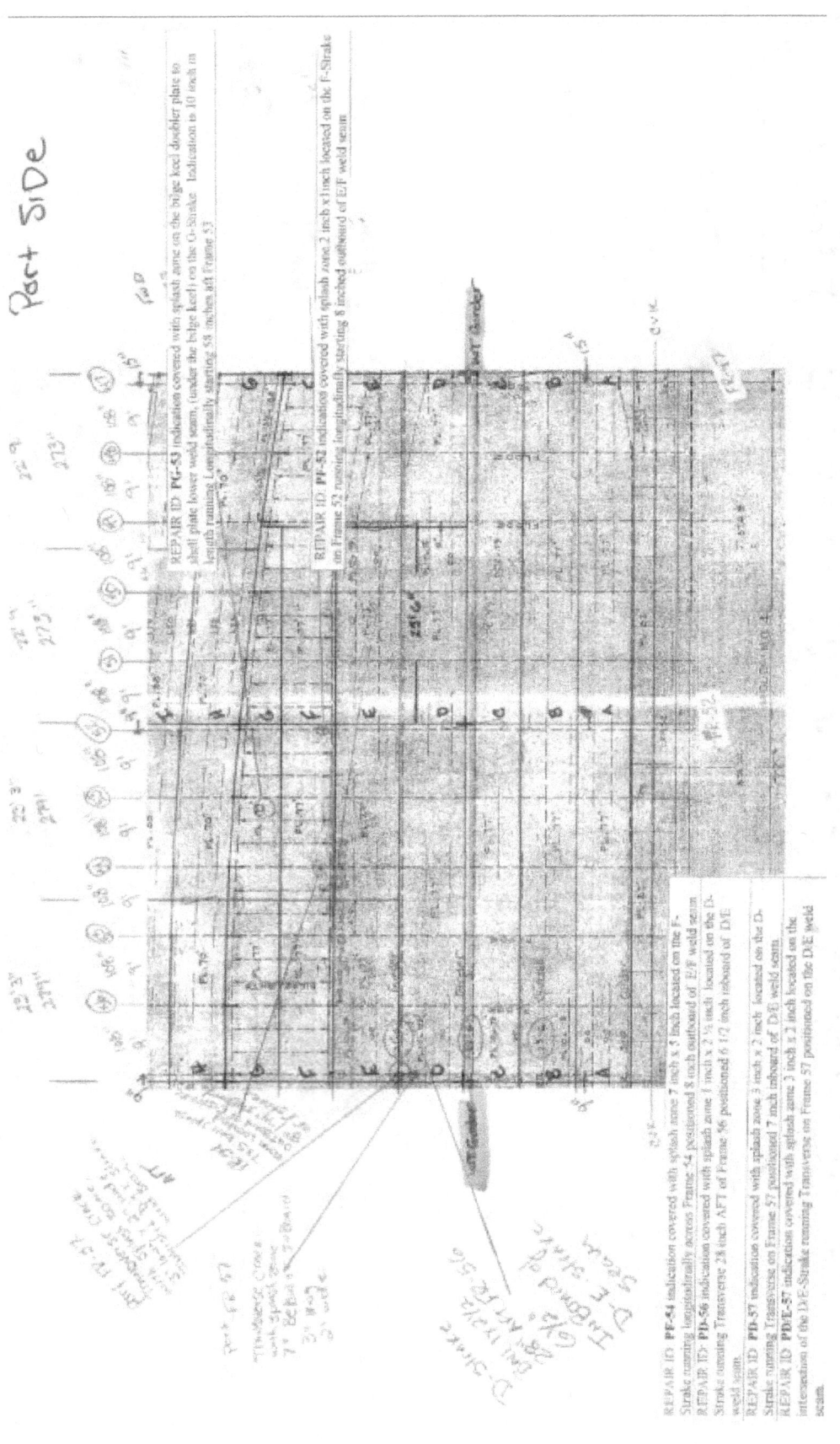

External Hull Survey: Port F57-FM

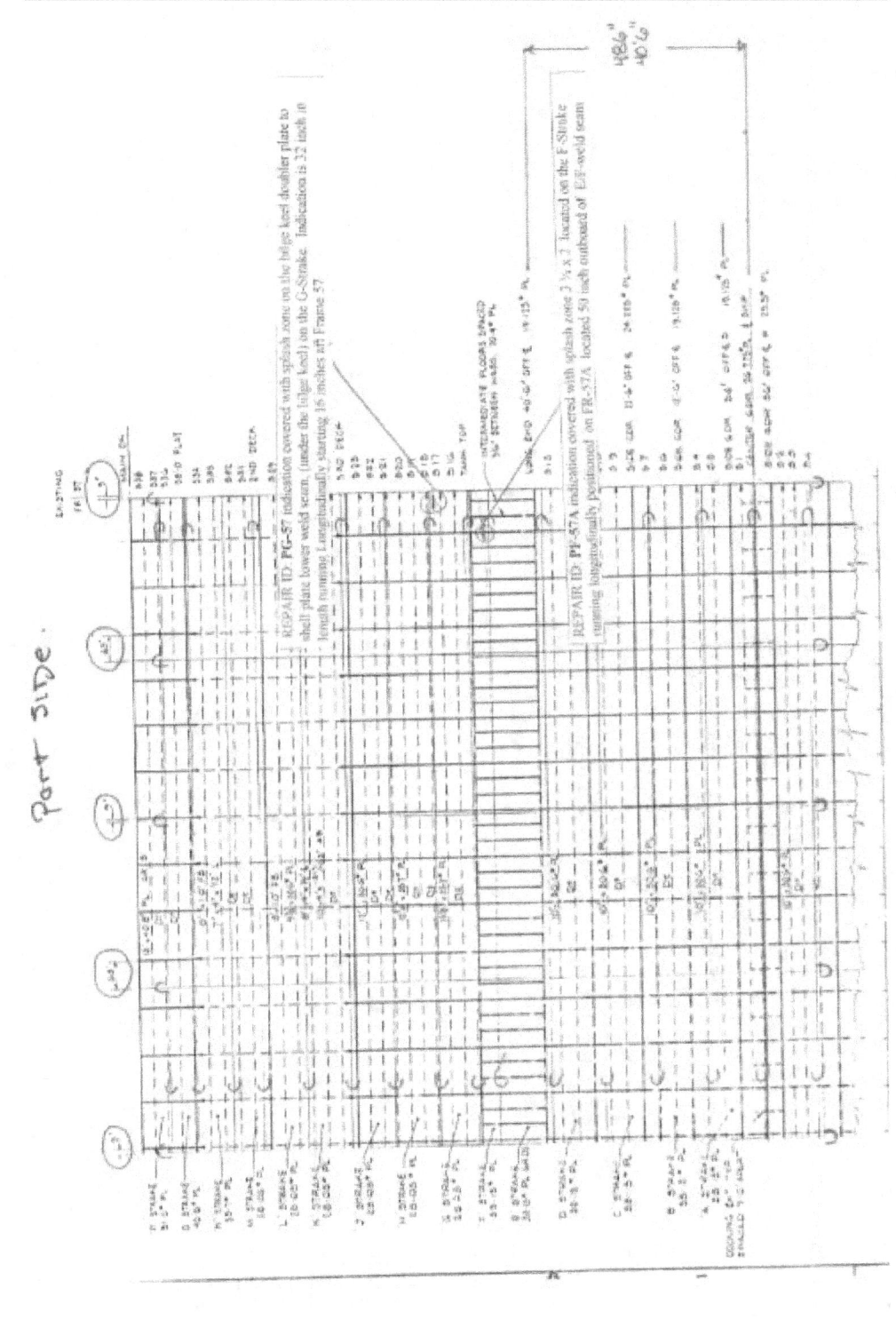

Post-Salvage Diving Ecological Assessment Survey Report
Grounding of USNS SGT. MATEJ KOCAK (T-AK 3005)
Okinawa, Japan, 22 January 2015

Submitted: 27 February 2015

Table of Contents

Executive Summary

On the morning of Thursday 22 January 2015 at approximately 11:30 during the ebb tide, USNS SGT. MATEJ KOCAK (T-AK 3005) ran hard aground on a reef off the East Coast of Okinawa, Japan. The vessel was ballasted down in place and remained grounded on a coral reef with a 1.5° port list for 12 days. On 3 February she was successfully refloated and sailed to East Navy pier at White Beach. Ship damage diving surveys carried out on the vessel identified damage to the starboard and port sides of MATEJ KOCAK's hull as a result of the grounding.

Five dive surveys were carried out by Naval Facilities (NAVFAC) Engineering and Expeditionary Warfare Center's (EXWC) Marine Resource Assessment Diving Services (MRADS), Polaris Applied Sciences, and Marentas / ECM on 7, 10 and 11 February 2015 to investigate and document damage on the reef as a result of the grounding. The dives were conducted both within the vessels grounding footprint and outside of the footprint to observe any possible ancillary damage, and compare the grounding scar to adjacent areas of the reef unaffected by the grounding incident. An AquaMap system was deployed to help accurately measure any observed impacts. In addition, GPS, cameras and transect tapes were used to document the reef dive survey. Dives were conducted over three days with a combined bottom time of 730 minutes.

The grounding site is on the edge of a fringing reef and consists of relict coral and limestone with high bathymetric variability. Colonies of live hard and soft corals, along with other benthic biota are present. Coral bleaching was evident throughout the reef, not just at the grounding site, indicating a recent previous bleaching event affected this area, although, bleaching was noticeably higher in areas underneath the ship after the salvage.

Dive surveys revealed that the hull crushed and scraped the seabed when the vessel grounded. The existing rugosity of the seabed resulted in scarred, patchy areas of damage to the reef on high relief features above 7 meters (20 ft), with large, un-impacted areas between the scars containing some rubble from the scarred areas. Four main scar areas were observed and hull contact damage within these areas ranged from 80 to 100%. The total area of these main damage footprints is approximately 640 m^2 (765 yd^2). Additionally there were some smaller partially scraped areas along the starboard side of the vessel and near one of the main scar areas. Theses partially scraped areas were likely only briefly impacted by the hull resulting in some fracturing of the coral and limestone reef. The damage in these areas range from 10 to 70% and cover approximately 33 m^2 (~40 yd^2). There was evidence of bottom paint in several discreet patches in the main scar areas. These patches were usually on the edges of the scar areas and ranged in size from 15cm (6 in) up to 1 m (39 in).

The obvious injuries that were a result of the removal of the vessel from the reef are two longer scrapes to the north of the grounding site, a rubble pile near the western most main scar, and 3 large tires near the stern on the port side. The northern scrapes are likely the result of anchors and/or lines from support vessels present on the port side of the vessel. These scrapes cover an area of approximately 50 m^2 but within that area only about 10% is damaged. Extensive searches could not positively identify damage due to the port anchor being dropped underfoot. No significant damage was found aft of the grounding site indicating the vessel took roughly the same route when extracted as when it was grounded.

A review and assessment of the grounding site and subsequent salvage operations suggests that biologically insignificant amounts of trace toxic metals were introduced to the environment and the discharge of foreign ballast water poses a negligible to undetectable environmental risk.

Incident Background

Circumstances of the incident

On the morning of Thursday 22 January 2015 at approximately 11:30 during ebb tide, USNS SGT. MATEJ KOCAK grounded at 26°12'1.00"N 127°56'7.00"E. (USNS SGT MATEJ KOCAK, Length x Breadth: 250.2 m X 32.2 m, Flag: USA (US), MMSI: 366203000, Call Sign: NKCK, Owners: U.S. Navy (Military Sealift Command), Operators: U.S. Transportation Command (TRANSCOM), Managers: Keystone, P&I Club: North of England). MATEJ KOCAK is a converted RO-RO container ship (Ex. Name: SS JOHN B. WATERMAN), delivered to MSC in the mid 1980s after which a shipyard conversion added 48m (157 ft) to the total length of the ship and a helicopter platform. MATEJ KOCAK is a government owned vessel currently operated by Keystone for Military Sealift Command (MSC) under TRANCOM.

After loading cargo and ammunition for Exercise COBRA GOLD (Thailand), MATEJ KOCAK ran aground exiting Okinawa harbor (Figure 1). The grounding caused neither personnel injuries nor oil pollution. MATEJ KOCAK was successfully refloated and moored alongside East Navy pier at White Beach on 3 February.

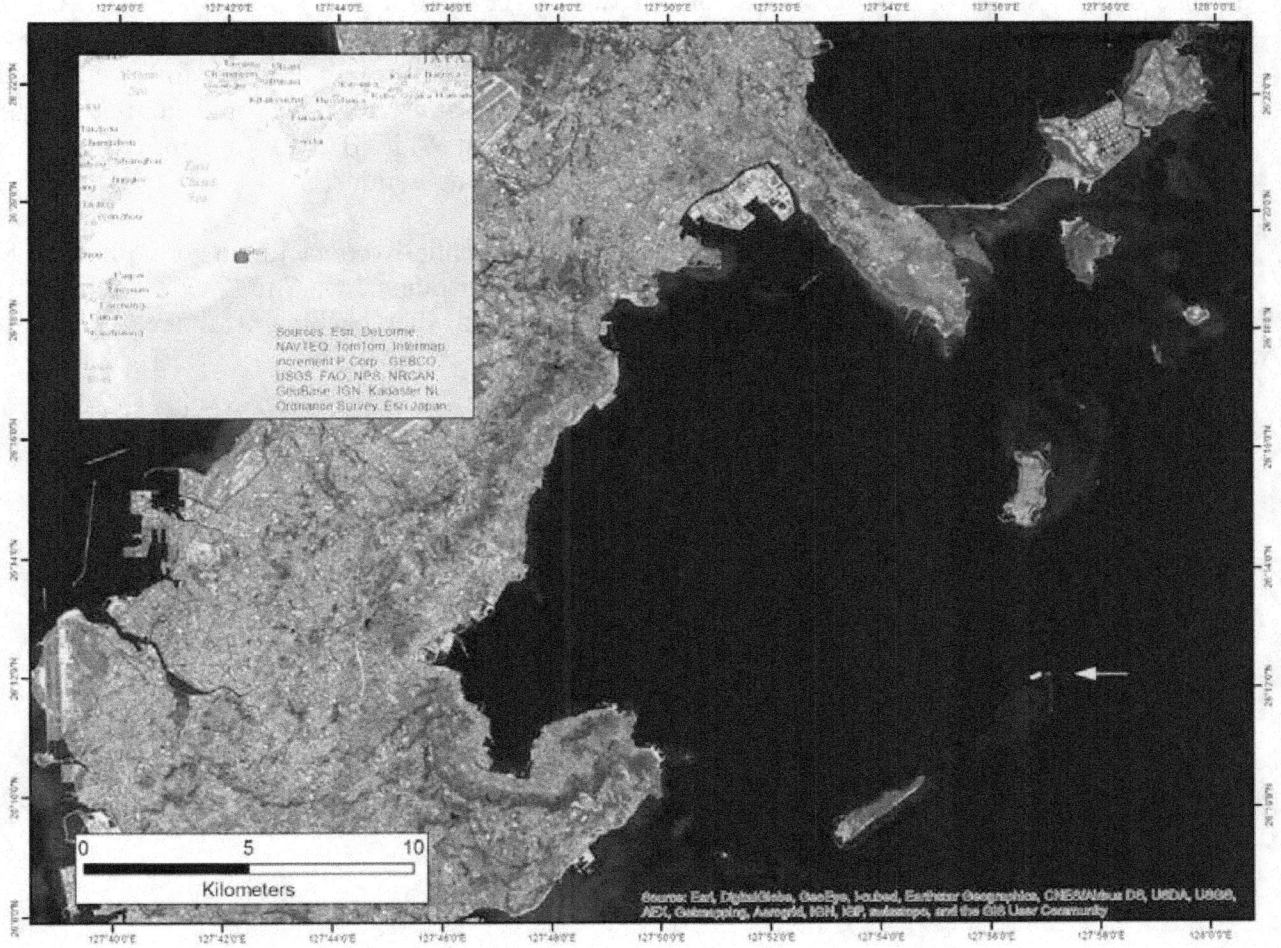

Figure 1. Overview of grounding site location.

Grounding and salvage

The vessel grounded on Uhu Bisi reef on 22 January 2015, touching bottom amidships alongside a shelf with forward and after parts afloat. Neither the bow nor stern and running gear contacted the reef. She remained hard aground throughout the tide cycle. Structural hull damage occurred as a result of the grounding. On the starboard side, indentation was found from Frame 37 to 57 and there is a large gash in the shell plate starting slightly after of Frame 50 and traveling to slightly forward of Frame 57. At its widest the gash width is 35.5 cm (14 in) with an average width of 20 cm (8 in). The gash is inside starboard double bottom saltwater ballast tanks #4. On the portside the structural damage encompasses #3 double bottom fixed ballast tank, #4 double bottom wing saltwater ballast tank and #4A double bottom fixed ballast tank. An unknown amount of dry magnetite and hematite fixed ballast was released as a result of the rupture.

While aground, the vessel's heading was 066 degrees and the list was to port at approximately 1.5 degrees. The vessel was described as lively enough to roll at high tide but static at low tide. The vessel ballasted down to remain stable on the reef, and dropped the port anchor. On 1 February Nippon Salvage barge MISHIMA moored to MATEJ KOCAK portside to be used as a 'fender' between MATEJ KOCAK and tanker SLNC PAX during fuel lightering operations (Figures 2 and 3). The three vessels configuration was formed with MATEJ KOCAK, MISHIMA and PAX, so that the tanker could remain in deeper water as her draft is deeper than MISHIMA's (4 m versus 7 m, 13 ft versus 20 ft). Fuel lightering began 2 February in the morning and was followed by de-ballasting the morning of 3 February. The vessel was successfully refloated on 3 February at the high tide and sailed under her own power to East Navy Pier at White Beach. An approximate total of 2000 tons of ballast water was released during the salvage operations.

During refloating there was concern for the running gear potentially contacting a coral pinnacle 80 cm (30 in) under the rudder (Figure 4) and propeller. Another pinnacle at 7 m (24 ft) depth off the port quarter was also noted as a potential hazard to be avoided when backing off the reef.

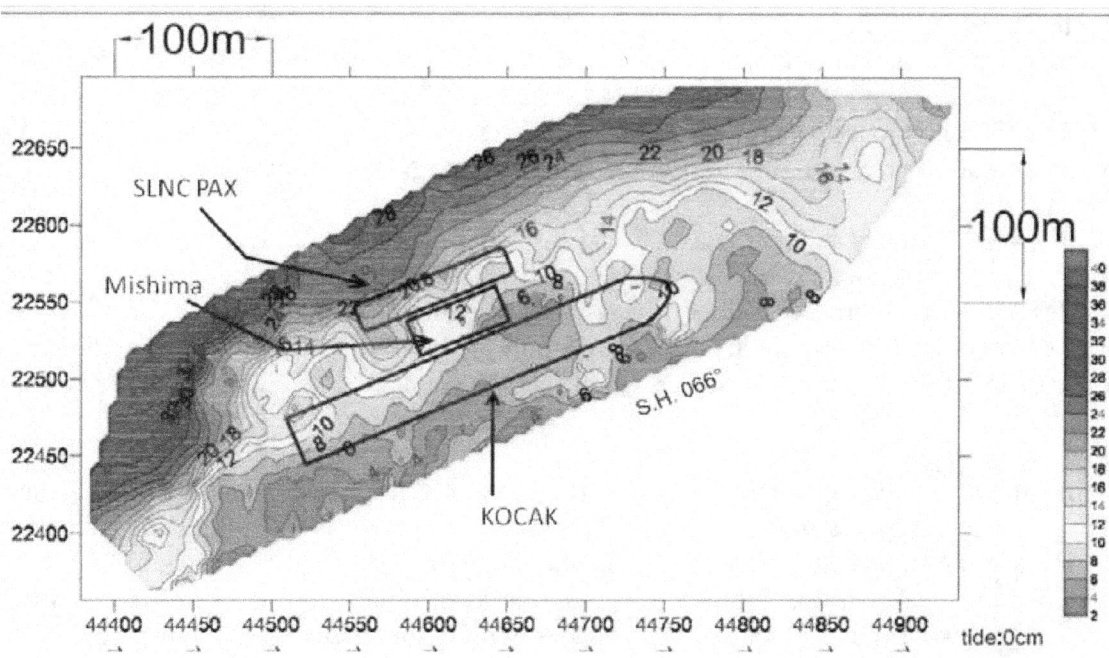

Figure 2. Positioning of MATEJ KOCAK, PAX and MISHIMA during fuel lightering and depth to sea bed (survey carried out by Nippon Salvage).

Figure 3. Overview of fuel lightering operations, where MISHIMA barge is used as a 'fender' between MATEJ KOCAK and SLNC PAX during fuel lightering operations. Tugs HEISEI MARU and NAKAGUSUKU MARU are onsite for salvage operations. Note port anchor underfoot. (2 February 2015).

Figure 4. Vessel rudder and propeller in relation to clearance on the reef.

General characteristics of the area

Okinawa Prefecture is the southernmost prefecture of Japan. It is composed of the Ryukyu Islands in a chain of hundreds of islands over 1,000 kilometres (620 miles) long, extending south-westerly towards Taiwan. Okinawa's capital, Naha, is located in the southern part of Okinawa Island along with the main international airport, a 1.5 hour drive to Nakagusuku Port.

MATEJ KOCAK ran aground off the East Coast of Okinawa, in the eastern portion of Nakagusuku Bay. This bay is located on the southern coast of Okinawa Island. The bay covers 220 km^2 (137 miles^2) with an average depth of 15 m (50 ft). It contains two islands, Kudaka Island and Tsuken Island. Tatsu Kuchi is the main sea entrance into the bay; it is 3 km (2 miles) wide and has a depth of 55 m (180 ft). Numerous large and small islands, reefs, and shoal waters bracket the entrance.

Okinawa is home to a variety of fauna and flora including IUCN listed Endangered marine mammals (the dugong, Steller's sea lion, and several mysticete whale species among them) and 5 species of sea turtles some of which lay their eggs in the southern islands of Okinawa. Okinawa and the many islands that make up the Prefecture contain areas of abundant coral reef habitat and the incident area is known for coral reefs. Okinawa is within the Indo-Pacific biogeographic region which contains the world's most diverse coral reef ecosystems. Spalding et al. (2001) lists 719 scleractinian coral species, 690 alcyonacean coral species and 4,000 fish species within the Indo-Pacific biogeographic region. In Okinawa approximately 400 species of corals and 1,000 species of fish have been identified (Reference 1). The fishing villages of Iheiya and Awase are also in the vicinity of the casualty.

The general location of Nakagusuku Bay is composed of a combination of man-made structures, seaweed cultivation facilities, sandy beaches, rocky outcrops and LNG / LPG and oil refinery facilities.

The vessel grounded on the outer NW edge of Uhu Bisi reef which stretches over 5 km (3 miles) in a NW – SE direction forming an inverted C curve, with a width ranging from 1 – 2 km (0.6 – 1.2 miles).

Reef Assessment Dives Post Vessel Removal

Dive surveys and methods

After the vessel was removed from the reef, two dive surveys were conducted on 7 February 2015 jointly with Polaris Applied Sciences, Inc. (Polaris) and Marentas/ECM. Naval Facilities (NAVFAC) Engineering and Expeditionary Warfare Center's (EXWC) Marine Resource Assessment Diving Services (MRADS) provided surface support to the surveys on 7 February from the contracted dive vessel, however did not enter the water in compliance with U.S. military dive regulations. On 10 February, a third dive was conducted with Polaris, Marentas/ECM and MRADS. The fourth dive was conducted on 10 February and one final dive on 11 February with MRADS only. The 10 and 11 February dives were supported by U.S. Army Special Forces divers from ODA 1115 and 1125, Alfa Company, First Battalion, First Special Forces Group diving from a U.S Army landing craft, utility (LCU) and supported by U.S. Navy rigid hulled inflatable boats (RHIBs) from Fleet Activities, Okinawa at White Beach. All together 5 dives were undertaken at the grounding location encompassing 730 minutes of bottom time.

The objective of the surveys was to identify grounding and removal injury and to collect general ecological information and photographs about the grounding site and surrounding reef area. The dives were conducted both within the vessels grounding footprint and outside of the footprint to observe any possible ancillary damage. An AquaMap SONAR system was deployed to help accurately measure any observed impacts and empirically define the size of the grounding scar.

AquaMap consists of 3 stationary transducers and a hand-held data collection transducer. The three baseline transducers are stationary units and are moored to the bottom of the ocean floor around the dive site. The diver station is a mobile transducer and is moved around the dive site to areas of interest. The diver station transmits a brief sonar signal (or sonar code), which travels to all three baseline stations. Upon receipt of a signal, each baseline station transmits a reply back to the diver station. The diver station is then able to compute its distance from each of the baseline stations. A relative coordinate system is developed and precise positions (between 15 cm (6 in) and 50 cm (20 in) based on wave/swell conditions) can be recorded within the dive site. Buoys attached to each of the baseline stations are geo-referenced with a GPS and these points can be used to place the area in a global reference, but the GPS position is not used when calculating distances and areas measured. In addition to the AquaMap, GPS, cameras and transect tapes were used to document the reef dive survey.

Description of surrounding reef
The grounding site is on the edge of a fringing reef and consists of relict coral and limestone with considerable bathymetric variability (rugosity). Colonies of live hard and soft corals, along with other benthic biota are present.

The depth range at the grounding site is approximately 6 to 8 meters (~18 to 24 ft) with a slope on the port side of the vessel's position rapidly dropping away to deeper depths. The cover of live soft corals, live hard corals, calcareous and fleshy algae varies from 10% to 50% with the higher concentrations on the slopes of the reef. Observed hard corals at the site include *Porities sp., Favia sp., Pachyseris speciosa, Goniastrea sp.* and *Acropora digitifera.* As a result of the wave activity present on the reef most of the corals were small in size (<30 cm, ~12 in), although there were a few larger colonies up to 1+ meters (3+ ft) in diameter, mainly in deeper water and along the steeper slopes. Soft corals at the site include *Millepora sp.* and *Sinularia sp.* Numerous other species were photographically documented.

Coral bleaching was evident throughout the reef indicating a previous bleaching event that affected this area. However, bleaching did seem to be higher near the grounding site, under the position of the vessel. If corals in the area were already naturally under stress, the shade from a vessel grounded for several weeks could cause others to become affected.

In addition to the hard and soft corals other organisms present at the site included a variety of sea stars (Asteroidea) and urchins (Echinoidea) , feather stars (*Oxycomanthus sp.* and other genera), sea anemones (Actiniaria), giant clams (*Tridacna* sp.) and a variety of reef-associated fish families. Characteristic photographs are shown in Figure 5.

Dive survey results

Based on surveyor dive surveys, the vessel made contact with the reef. As the vessel grounded this area of the hull crushed and scraped the coral reef in several locations (Figure 6). The rugosity of the reef resulted in the scarred areas being patchy with the reef between the impact areas healthy or containing some rubble from the scarred areas (Table 1). Four main scar areas were observed with these areas ranging from 80 to 100% damaged (Figure 7 A,B,C). The total area of these main scar areas is approximately 640 m^2 (765 yd^2). A smaller scar near the stern is approximately 12 m^2 (14 yd^2).

Additionally there were some smaller partially scraped areas along the starboard side of the vessel and near one of the main scar areas (Figure 7D). Theses partially scraped areas were likely briefly impacted by the hull resulting in some fracturing of the coral and limestone reef. The damage in these areas ranges from 10 up to 70% and covers approximately 33 m^2 (~40 yd^2).

While there is rubble to some extent near all the main scars, there are two more well defined rubble piles near the center of the impact area, and one on the starboard side of the westernmost scar (Figure 7E). These rubble piles cover an area of approximately 85 m^2 (~102 yd^2).

There was evidence of bottom paint in several discrete patches in the main scar areas (Figure 7F). These patches were usually on the edges of the scar areas and ranged in size from 15 cm (~6 inches) up to 1 m (~3 ft).

The only obvious injuries that were a result of the removal of the vessel from the reef are two longer scrapes to the north of the grounding site and a rubble pile near the western most main scar. The northern scrapes are in deeper water (13-15 m / 42 – 50 ft) than the main grounding site and are very narrow (1-2 m wide, ~3-6 ft) and linear (Figure 8A). These are possibly the result of anchors and/or lines from support vessels that were present on the port side of the vessel. These scrapes cover an area of approximately 50 m^2 (~60 yd^2) but within that area only about 10% is damaged. The rubble pile near the western most main scar is generally smaller and finer rubble and is covering the slope leading down from the main scar (Figure 8B). This rubble likely originated at the main scar area and was dragged backwards by the vessel as it was removed. This rubble pile covers an area of approximately 45 m^2 (~54 yd^2). Additionally, 3 tires were found on the port side between the stern and mid-ship, these are most likely from a barge or tug (Figure 8C). One final small pile of reef rubble approximately 9 m^2 (~ 11 yd^2) aft of the main site was identified, and likely caused by reef material embedded in the hull dropping free of the vessel during extraction (Figure 8D). After extensive searching, no damage was located where the port anchor was deployed underfoot, indicating whatever scarring was caused by the anchor is so minor that it could not be discerned from normal environmental conditions at the site.

Table 1. Summary of injury, source and area affected as determined from assessment dives.

Injury Description	Likely Injury Source	Approx. % Injury	Area
Main Scars (4 large/1 small)	Hull contact with reef	80-100%	652 m^2 (779 yd^2)
Partial Scrapes/Fracturing	Brief hull contact	10-70%	33 m^2 (40 yd^2)
Rubble Piles Near Scars	Vessel scraping coral/reef	30-75%	85 m^2 (102 yd^2)
Northern Scrapes	Lines/anchors from support vessels	10%	50 m^2 (60 yd^2)
Rubble Pile (western scar)	Debris deposited as vessel was removed	75%	45 m^2 (54 yd^2)
Rubble Pile (aft of main area)	Debris deposited as vessel was removed	75%	9m^2 (11 yd^2)
3 Tires Near Stern	Flotsam from support vessels	-	-

Figure 5. A) typical reef relief common at site, B) standard coral size (<30 cm, ~12 inches), C) a bleached coral next to a live coral, D) live coral cover and size present on deeper/slope areas, E) anemone (*Actiniaria*) near grounding site, F) giant clam (*Tridacna* sp.) found near grounding site.

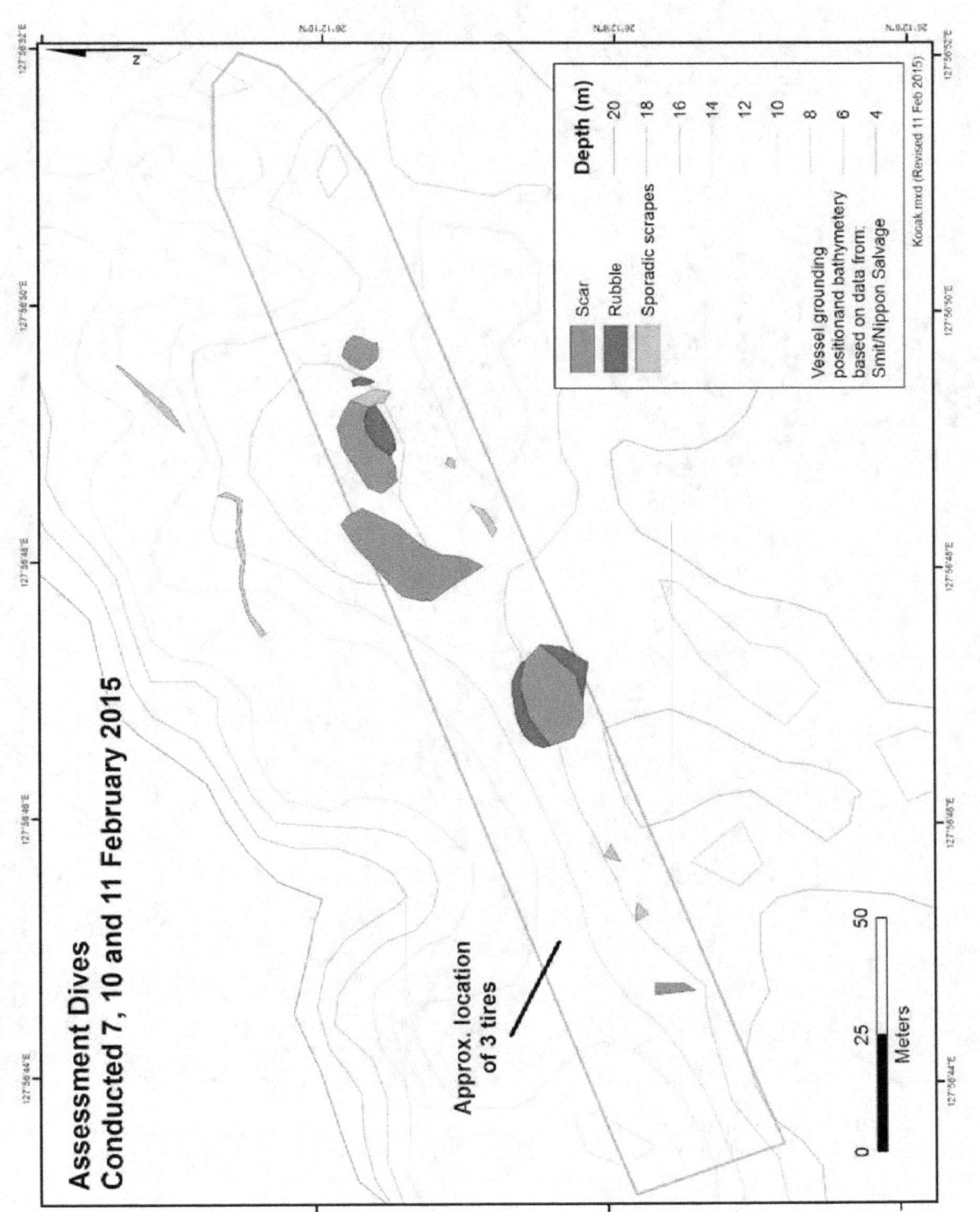

Figure 6. Delineated impacts at grounding site.

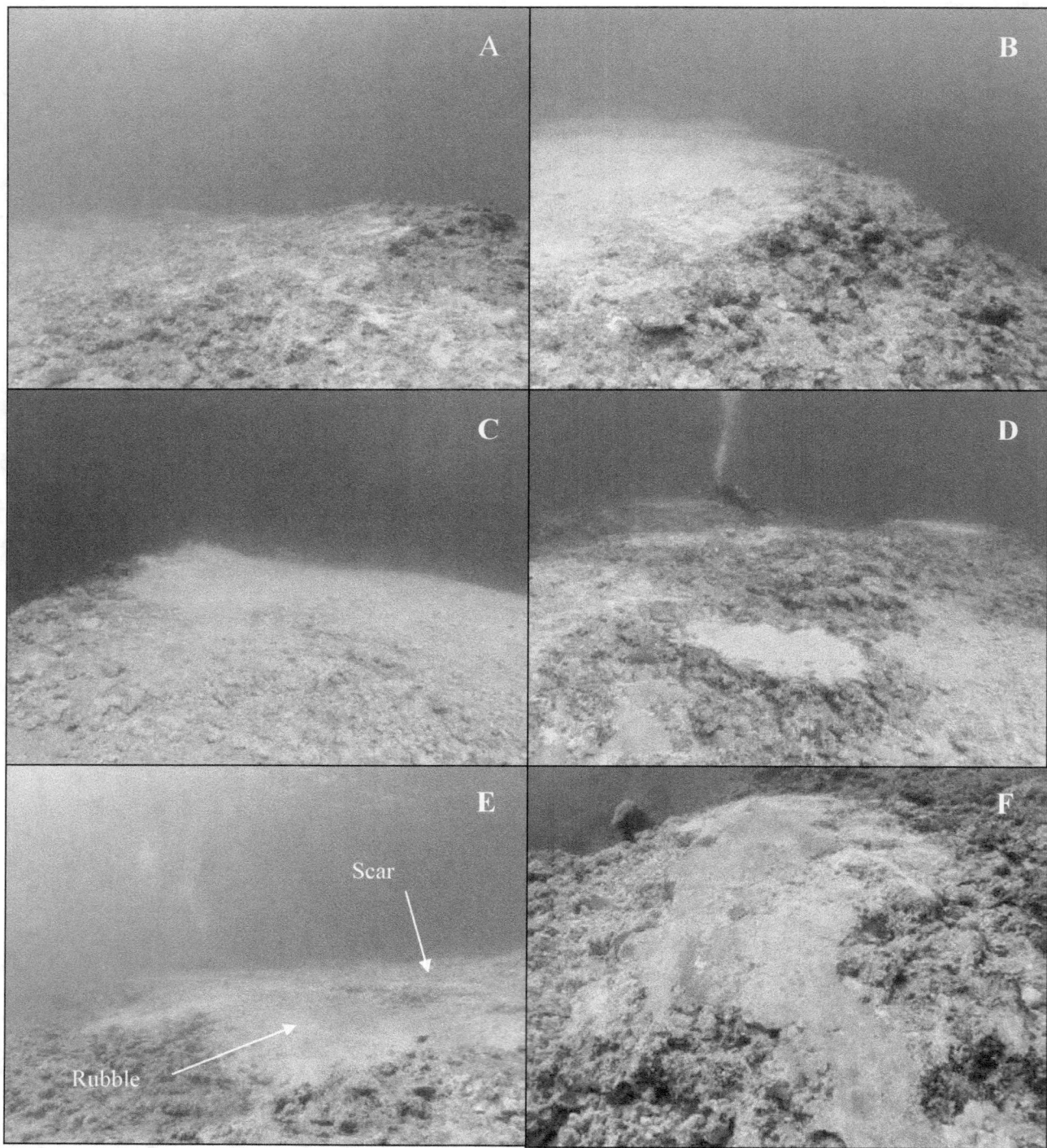

Figure 7. A, B and C) crushed and broken coral/limestone in main scar areas, D) patchy, partially scraped areas in between main scar areas, E) larger, defined rubble pile next to scar area, F) hull paint on reef.

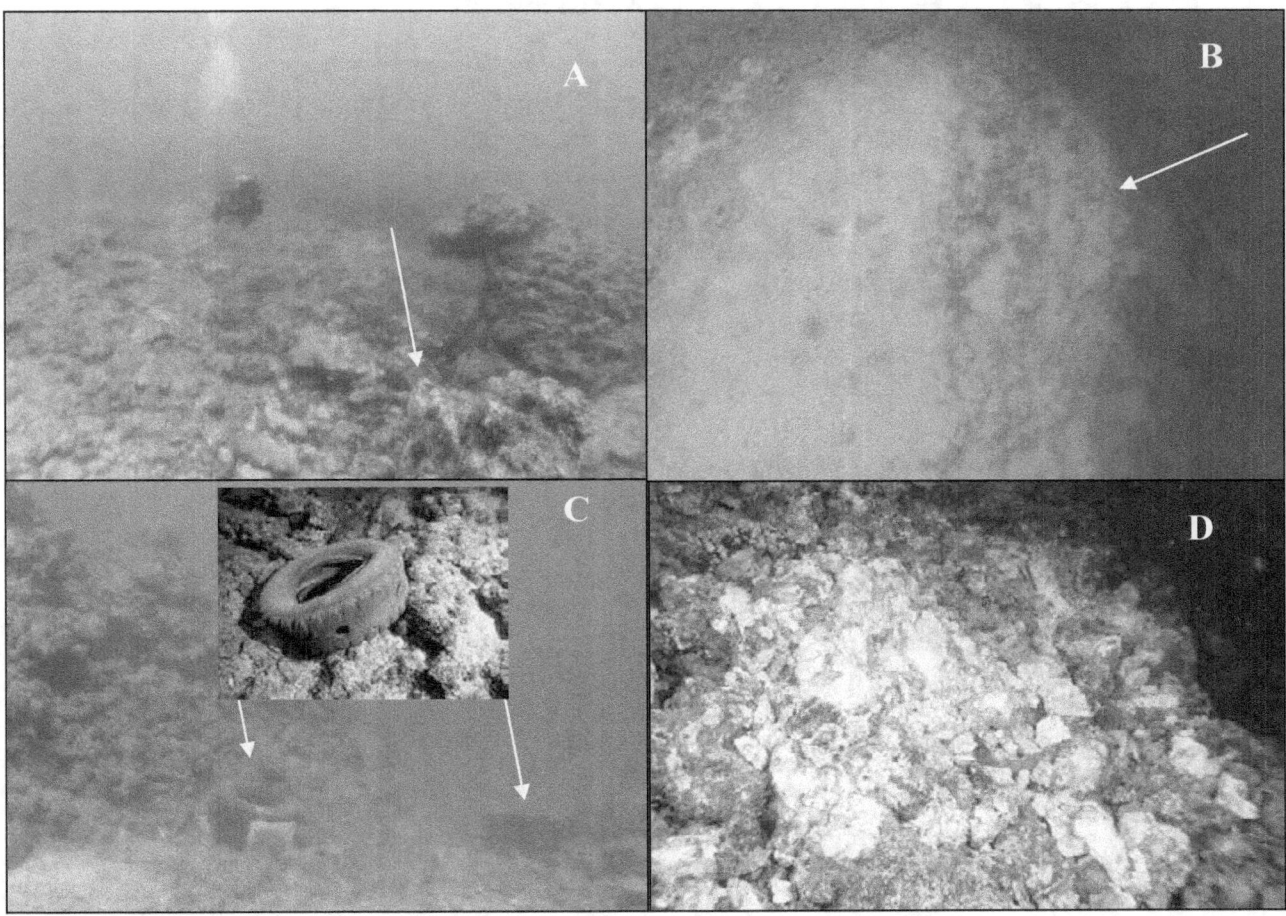

Figure 8. A) long, linear scrapes to the north of the grounding site, B) small, fine rubble pile covering slope off of a main scar area, C) tires on the reef, likely from a barge or tug, D) rubble pile likely originating from reef material lodged in the hull then subsequently deposited on the reef.

Additional Environmental Considerations

Ballast water

After informing Japanese Coast Guard officials, approximately 2000 tons of ballast water were discharged from MATEJ KOCAK into the sea in order to create enough buoyancy to reduce grounding force reaction of the hull, and allow for successful extraction of the vessel.

During refloating operations, ballast water was discharged from #1 deep, forepeak and a smaller amount from #5 inner bottom outboard on 3 February. The #5 inner bottom outboard was loaded on 2 February at grounding location in Nakagusuku Bay and is therefore 'local'. The #1 deep and forepeak were exchanged in the mid-Atlantic on 12 and 15 August 2014.

It is common knowledge that ships are a major vector for the introduction of alien marine organisms. However, in Japan no species have been introduced solely by ballast water due to the fact that ballast water is usually retained within the ship for long enough to kill the organisms within it (Reference 2). The low importance of ballast water as a vector is a common feature among importers of natural resources such as Japan (Reference 3). The risk in the case of the MATEJ KOCAK grounding is further limited by the fact that the ballast water aboard originated from the open ocean thousands of kilometers away from Japan. Notably, the most significant source regions for species introduced to Japan are the North East Pacific and the East Asian Sea (Reference 2), and Japan is a net exporter of marine invasive species. The risk that MATEJ KOCAK salvage introduced alien invasive species to Okinawan waters through ballast water discharge is therefore insignificant.

Dry ballast

An undetermined amount of dry ballast material was released from the vessel as a result of hull penetration due to the grounding. According to the Material Safety Data Sheet (MSDS) provided by the manufacturer (Ballast Technologies, Inc.) magnetite and hematite ballast is composed of approximately 95% iron (Fe) and iron mineral (Fe_2O_3, Fe_2O_4) dusts. The material contains traces of heavy metal elements, and as listed on the MSDS may contain a copper content of < 0.1 % and a chromium content of $< 0.02\%$ by weight. The iron is quickly chelated by bacteria and its bioavailability and toxicity is very low.

The bioavailability of the chemicals is the dry ballast is unknown. If copper is bioavailable it remains at lower taxonomic levels, and is not assessed to accumulate in higher trophic levels (Reference 4). In fish, muscle tissue has been found to have very little capacity for chromium accumulation and all available evidence suggests that chromium is not biomagnified in marine environments (References 5 and 6). As such, the total amount of trace copper and chromium released as a result of this incident is highly unlikely to cause a toxicity hazard to fish collected for human consumption. Given that reef survey dives were not able to locate any substantial deposit or concentration of this material on the sea floor in over 700 minutes of bottom searching and that exceedance of current national chronic Cu WQC (3.1 µg/L dissolved) is not necessarily indicative of bioavailability or toxicity to biota (Reference 7), it is assessed that the overall environmental impact of the dry ballast release is negligible to undetectable.

Anti-fouling paint

At all points the ship's hull contacted the reef, the anti-fouling paint was abraded and deposited in the contact scar. According to the certificate from PPG Protective and Marine Coatings, the TBT-free antifouling coating ABC 3 (EPA Reg. Nr. 7313-18) was applied on the underwater area of the vessel during 11-7 to 12-7, 2011 at Bayonne Dry Dock, Bayonne N.J. ABC 3 complies with the IMO Convention on the control of Harmful Antifouling Systems on Ships of 2001 (AFS/CONF/26). ABC 3 is a one component, high performance self-polishing antifouling, containing the active biocide Copper (1) oxide. The biocide is bound to the polymeric matrix and is released by hydrolysis at the paint surface. The rate of release is controlled and constant, depending on water movement. Microscopic matrix layers are continuously washed away when the ship is moving, exposing new active layers. The life of SPC usually ranges between 4 and 5 years (Reference 8), indicating the paint on MATEJ KOCAK was nearing the end of its effectiveness at the time of the grounding incident. Given the previously discussed non-bioavailability of copper compounds at higher trophic levels (copper is lipophilic and only shows a slight tendency towards bioaccumulation) (Reference 9), the presence of some anti-fouling paint on the reef in the grounding scar presents an environmental profile that remains consistent with current environmental quality standards (Reference 9), and is therefore not assessed to be a significant hazard.

References

[1]   Spalding, M.D., Green, E.P., Ravilious, C. 2001. *World Atlas of Coral Reefs*. University of California Press. 423 pp.

[2]   Koike, F., Clout, M. N., Kawamichi, M., De Poorter, M. and Iwatsuki, K. (eds). 2006. *Assessment and control of biological invasion risks*. Published by SHOUKADOH Book Sellers, Kyoto, Japan and the World Conservation Union (IUCN), Gland, Switzerland. 216pp.

[3]   Otani, M. *Important vectors for marine organisms unintentionally introduced to Japanese waters*. 2006. In Koike, F., Clout, M.N., Kawamichi, M., De Poorter, M. and Iwatsuki, K. (eds), Assessment and Control of Biological Invasion Risks. Shoukadoh Book Sellers, Kyoto, Japan and IUCN, Gland, Switzerland. Pp. 92-103.

[4]   Seligmen, P. and Zirino, A. (eds). 1998. *Chemistry, toxicity, and bioavailability of copper and its relationship to regulation in the marine environment*. Technical Document 3044 Office of Naval Research Workshop Report. Space and Naval Warfare Systems Center San Diego, CA.

[5]   Oana, P. 2006. *Chromium impact on marine ecosystem*. USAMVB Timisoara, Calea Aradului 119, 200645 Timisoara. (63) pp. 379-384.

[6]   Eisler, R. 1986. *Chromium hazards to fish, wildlife, and invertebrates: a synoptic review*. U.S.   Fish and Wildlife Service Biological Report 85 (1.6). 60 pp).

[7]   Rosen, G. Et Al. *Effects of copper on marine invertebrate larvae in surface water from San Diego Bay, CA*. SPAWAR Systems Center San Diego, CA Computer Sciences Corporation

[8]   Terlizzia, A. Et Al. 2001. *Environmental impact of antifouling technologies: state of the art and perspectives*. Aquatic Conser. Mar. Freshw. Ecosyst. 11: 311–317.

[9]   Almeida, E. Et. Al. 2007. *Marine paints: the particular case of antifouling paints*. Progress in Organic Coatings 59: 2–20.

UNDERWATER SHIP HUSBANDRY
OPERATIONS REPORT

USNS SGT. MATEJ KOCAK (T-AK 3005)
DAMAGE ASSESSMENT AND HULL REPAIR

USNS SGT. MATEJ KOCAK (T-AK 3005)

DAMAGE ASSESSMENT AND HULL REPAIR

FEBRUARY 2015

PERFORMED FOR:
Department of the Navy
Naval Sea Systems Command (SEA 00C5)
1333 Isaac Hull Ave. SE (Stop 1075)
Washington Navy Yard, DC 20376

UNDER:
Contract N00024-11-D-4115
Delivery Order 0125
PIHI - 15019

BY:
Phoenix International Holdings, Inc.
9301 Largo Drive West
Largo, MD 20774
301.341.7800

EXECUTIVE SUMMARY

In January 2015, the Supervisor of Salvage and Diving, Underwater Ship Husbandry Division (Code 00C5) of the Naval Sea Systems Command (NAVSEA) directed Phoenix International Holdings, Inc. (Phoenix) to perform damage assessment and hull repair to USNS Sgt. Matej Kocak (T-AK 3005). The work was performed under contract N00024-11-D-4115 Delivery Order (D.O.) 0125, at Naval Station White Beach, Okinawa. On site project management was performed by NAVSEA Technical Representative, Jacob Nessel 00C59. No Third Party Monitor was required for the emergent repairs to USNS Sgt. Matej Kocak.

On 22 January 2015, USNS Sgt. Matej Kocak ran aground exiting Okinawa Harbor. Initial damage control and removal from the reef was completed by Smit Salvage subcontractor Nippon Salvage. On 3 February 2015, the ship was removed from the reef and transported to East Navy Pier, Berth 1, at Naval Facility White Beach (NFWB). Nippon Salvage conducted a survey of the hull, and patched damaged areas with a "Splash Zone" type epoxy.

On 3 February, Phoenix personnel arrived at NFWB. On 4 February, repair equipment arrived and Phoenix attended a meeting with key personnel to discuss vessel unload and repair operations. Phoenix conducted a detailed survey of exterior damaged areas identified by Nippon Salvage. Damaged areas were then designated and identified utilizing the following ID system: Port or Starboard (P/S) strake (Alpha) designation-nearest frame. Nine indications on the port side were located: PE-45, PF-52, PG-53, PF-54, PD-56, PD-57, PD-57I, PG-57, and PF-57A. Additionally on the starboard side, a large hull breach was identified and surveyed.

Interior damaged areas were designated and identified utilizing the following ID system: Port or Starboard (P/S)-nearest frame-inboard or outboard (I/O)-repair number (if applicable). Three damaged areas were located in Cargo Hold 3A. PI-47-1 and PI-47-3 were separate fractures in the deck plate around two vertical bulkhead stiffeners along the transverse bulkhead. The PI-47-2 fracture was located in the deck plate, outboard and forward of the Fixed Ballast Tank 3A access. The following seven damaged areas were located in Cargo Hold 4A: PI-52, PI-57, PI-57O, PI-57I, PI-57 Corner Repair, Cargo Hold 4A watertight door, and PI-57A. Note that the door was non-operational due to hogging of the deck under the door, which caused the door to be displaced upward along the sealing surface resulting in a complete loss of water tight integrity on the bottom sealing surface. Detailed descriptions of interior and exterior damage are located in Appendix B, Condition Found Reports.

After port and starboard exterior damaged areas were surveyed, a repair plan was developed. Metal samples were harvested from all potential repair areas and sent to the lab for composition analysis. Dome patches were selected to repair PF-54 (12-inch diameter) and PD-56 (8-inch diameter). Elliptical box patches were selected to repair PE-45 (41-inches long by 8-inches wide), PD-57 (13-inches long by 5-inches wide), and PD-57I (10-inches long by 6-inches wide).

For each repair site the crack or indication was either arrested or cropped out with a carbon arc cutter. A patch was then templated and cut to the contour of the hull. Once proper fit up was achieved, the patch was tacked in place and welded out in accordance with (iaw) Phoenix's ABS approved WPS-202-W-ABS Rev. 3 or WPS-404-W Rev. 2.

No damage to the hull shell plate was noted on indications PG-53 and PG-57. Damage was localized to the bilge keel doubler plate and the fractured welds were faired out with a hydraulic grinder. PF-57A and PF-52 were deemed irrelevant and no repairs were made.

No attempt was made to seal the starboard hull breach. The breach was crack arrested in multiple locations utilizing a carbon arc cutter.

After the port hull shell plate was sealed, work began on interior repairs. Damaged areas PI-47-2, PI-52, PI-57A, PI-57O, PI-57, PI-57-I were repaired with weld buildup or weld replacement. For these repairs damaged areas were ground down to clean white metal, and welded iaw Phoenix's ABS approved dry welding procedure WPS-101-D Rev. 2. Repairs along a weld seam were tied into the existing weld.

For repairs on the Cargo Hold 4A watertight door, four heavy dogs were cut to release the door. The lower portion of the door was removed and a 1/2-inch thick plate was templated to the contour of the damaged deck. After proper fit up was achieved, the Cargo Hold 4A watertight door was welded to the deck iaw WPS-101-D.

In Cargo Hold 3A, damaged areas PI-47-1 and PI-47-3 were repaired by welding a 1/4-inch thick collar or doubler plates around the base of the vertical bulkhead stiffeners. For these repairs the damaged areas were ground down and faired in. Collar plates were cut and bent to fit the contour of the damaged deck plate. Then the plates were welded in place iaw WPS-101-D.

Finally, damaged area PI-57 Corner was repaired with the installation of a 1/2-inch thick doubler plate. For this repair the damaged area was ground down and faired in. The doubler plate was templated to cover the damaged area and welded in place iaw WPS-101-D.

Prior to production underwater welding, divers satisfactorily welded confirmation plates using WPS-202-W-ABS Rev. 3 and WPS-404-W Rev. 2. The root passes and completed underwater welds were inspected by Level II NDT inspectors using Phoenix's NAVSEA approved Underwater Wet Magnetic Particle Testing (PII-UWMT) Method and Underwater Visual Testing (PII-UWVT) Method iaw American Welding Society (AWS) 3.6M 2010, Ch. 9. Surface welds were completed iaw WPS-101-D-ABS Rev. 2. All completed surface welds were inspected using Phoenix's Dry and Dry Chamber Magnetic Particle Testing (PII-D&DCMT) Method and Dry and Dry Chamber Visual Testing (PII-D&DCVT) Method iaw AWS D1.1 M-2010 (6.10). All repair areas were documented with video and still photography.

No Departures From Specification were submitted in support of this repair.

Repair team personnel performed 141.7 hours of bottom time without any accidents or injuries. A total of 7.9 linear feet of Underwater Mild Steel, 11.4 linear feet of High Nickel, and 64.7 linear feet of Surface Mild Steel welds were deposited to perform this repair. USNS Sgt. Matej Kocak personnel were responsive and provided valuable assistance throughout repair operations.

TABLE OF CONTENTS

1.0 BACKGROUND

In January 2015, MSC (Military Sealift Command) requested assistance from NAVSEA 00C5 to perform the damage assessment and hull repair on USNS Sgt. Matej Kocak (T-AK 3005). Phoenix International Holdings, Inc. was tasked by NAVSEA 00C5 to accomplish the work.

On 22 January 2015 at 1110 local time, after loading cargo and ammunition for exercise Cobra Gold, USNS Sgt. Matej Kocak ran aground exiting Okinawa Harbor. Smit Salvage and subcontracted Nippon Salvage assisted in damage control efforts and removed the vessel from the reef.

On 4 February 2015, Nippon Salvage conducted a survey of the hull, and patched damaged areas.

2.0   CHRONOLOGY

Monday 27, January. Phoenix received a verbal delivery order from NAVSEA.

Tuesday 28, January. The Process Control Work Package (PCWP) was developed.

Thursday, 29 January. The PCWP was submitted to NAVSEA.

Monday, 2 February. Five Phoenix personnel traveled from their respective Phoenix facilities to Okinawa, Japan. USNS Sgt. Matej Kocak was assisted and arrived at East Navy Pier, Berth 1. Phoenix Personnel arrived in Naha, Okinawa, and were transported to NSWB.

Tuesday, 3 February. Four Phoenix personnel traveled from their respective Phoenix facilities to Okinawa, Japan. All personnel arrived in Naha, Okinawa, and were transported to NSWB.

Wednesday, 4 February. The Phoenix Diving Supervisor, Technical Writer, and NAVSEA Technical Representative attended an 1100 meeting to discuss vessel unload and repair operations. Phoenix was informed that an ammunition offload would begin at 0800 on 4 February. Nippon Salvage conducted a hull survey, to assess damage after removal from the reef. Repair equipment from Norfolk, Virginia and Honolulu, Hawaii was delivered to the East Navy Pier.

Thursday, 5 February. Phoenix began receiving subcontracted repair support equipment. The Air Transportable Underwater Welding System One (ATUWS 1) arrived at the East Navy Pier. The diving system was unloaded, and Phoenix personnel began establishing the dive station along the starboard side of USNS Sgt. Matej Kocak. The Phoenix Diving Supervisor, Technical Writer, and NAVSEA Technical Representative attended a repair meeting onboard the ship and inspected the damaged internal areas. The diver's safety tags were hung, and the scope of diving operations was discussed with the Chief Engineer.

Friday, 6 February. Annual and biannual pre-operational maintenance was conducted on ATUWS I. Work continued establishing the dive station. The Work Authorization Form (WAF) was opened and the Memorandum of Agreement (MOA) was signed. NSWB Port Operations provided a platform to launch and recover divers. Laying out of reference lines and mapping damaged areas on the port side Frame 37 through Frame 57 Strakes A and B began. The exact locations of nine indications covered in a "Splash Zone" type epoxy compound (PE-45, PF-52, PG-53, PF-54, PD-56, PD-57, PD-57I, PF-57A, and PG-57) were mapped. A large hull breach on the starboard side was also mapped out. The damage spanned from 58-inches aft of Frame 50 at the F/G Strake longitudinal weld seam to 38-inches forward of Frame 57 in the G Strake. The breach was 14-inches at its widest point and had an average width of 8-inches. All damaged areas on the port side were covered in a "Splash Zone" type material so exact dimensions of damage could not be taken.

Saturday, 7 February. Completed the detailed inspection of damage on the port and starboard side. The Phoenix Diving Supervisor attended a repair meeting with NAVSEA. A repair plan was designed for indications on the port side and the large hull breach on the starboard side. Reference lines were laid out to map out the large box patch that would cover the starboard hull breach. Metal samples were taken from four locations on the starboard side. The delayed San Diego shipment of repair equipment was delivered. Phoenix began sourcing patch material with certifications, however all suppliers were closed for the weekend.

Sunday, 8 February. Metal samples were taken for all port indications and the starboard hull breach. A template was manufactured for the box patch to cover the starboard hull breach. The template was employed to ensure proper patch dimensions. Dimensions and templating results were sent to Phoenix engineers for box patch design.

Monday, 9 February. All metal samples were sent to Decisive Testing in San Diego, California for composition analysis. Phoenix continued working with local vendors to supply doubler plate material, however material with certifications was not available in Okinawa. Doubler plate material was located on mainland Japan from Sumitomo Shipyards. However as the material would not arrive for a minimum of four days, work began sourcing alternate suppliers. Phoenix inspection divers removed splash zone material and began UWVT and UWMT inspections on indication PE-45 (fracture, 35-inches long by 3/32-inches average width, with a maximum of 1/8-inches). On the interior of the ship, four heavy dogs on the water tight door in Cargo Hold 4A were burned off, to facilitate vehicle offload.

Tuesday, 10 February. Completed UWMT and UWVT inspections of indication PE-45 and began PF-52 (weak indication, 3/8-inches long by 1/64-inches wide). Work began gouging circular crack arrests on both ends of the longitudinal linier indication in the port Outboard Fixed Ballast Tank 3. Three large circular crack arrests were gauged in the starboard Outboard Fixed Ballast Tank 3 along the longitudinal hull breach. Additionally, a large crack arrest removed a 6-inch transverse indication in the starboard Outboard Fixed Ballast Tank 3. The indication was located 7-inches inboard of the longitudinal hull breach. Phoenix received guidance from NAVSEA to fly out two additional welders in support of (iso) internal dry welding repairs.

Wednesday, 11 February. Metal samples sent to San Diego were delivered for material composition analysis. Completed UWMT and UWVT inspections on indications PG-53 (fractured fillet weld on the bilge keel doubler plate), PF-54 (fracture, 6-inches long by 1-1/2-inches wide), PD-56 (fracture, 5/8-inches long by 1/32-inches wide), PD-57 (micro fractures, 9-3/4-inch long by 3-1/4-inch wide area), PD-57I (micro fractures, 4-1/2-inch long by 3/4-inch wide area), PG-57 (fractured fillet weld on the bilge keel doubler plate), and PF-57A (weak indication). With inspection of damaged areas complete, Addendum I (Repair Plan) to the PCWP was drafted. Indications would either be repaired with a doubler plate or a dome or elliptical patch. Crack arrests were gouged on linear indications located between FR-37 thru FR-47 on the port Outboard J Non-Fixed Ballast Tank 4. Linear indications located aft of FR-57 on the port Outboard Fixed Ballast Tank 4A were also gouged to arrest further crack development. A San Diego shipment containing floating umbilicals and elliptical patches was received. Crack arrest gauging was continued on starboard Outboard Ballast J-tank 4 along the 55-foot 9-inch hull breach. Phoenix would make no attempt to seal the starboard hull breach per direction of NAVSEA. Indications PF-52 and PF-57A were surface gouges in the shell plate and identified as non relevant indications. Repairs would not be made to these indications. Additionally, indications PG-53 and PG-57 would not be repaired since they were located on the bilge keel base plate weld seam. In the case of these damaged areas the shell plate separated from the base plate of the bilge keel, no breach in the shell plate was located.

Thursday, 12 February. Metal sample composition analysis results were received. Based on the Carbon Equivalent and Carbon values Phoenix ABS approved welding procedures WPS-404-W Rev. 2 and WPS-202-W-ABS Rev. 3 were selected for this repair. Four Phoenix welder divers completed welding of confirmation plates to both procedures in the 4F position. Two additional Phoenix topside welders arrived in Naha, Okinawa and were transported to NSWB. A 12-inch elliptical patch was fit up, templated, and seal welded iaw WPS-202-W-ABS to repair PF-54. An 8-inch elliptical patch was selected to repair PD-56. This patch was fit up, templated, and the root weld was started iaw and WPS-404-W.

Friday, 13 February. Seal welding on PD-56 was completed. UWMT and UWVT inspections were completed on PD-56 and PF-54, results were acceptable. Fabrication of doubler plates for repair sites PE-45, PD-57 and PD-57I was completed. The PE-45 doubler plate was converted to a elliptical box doubler to fit compound curvature of the hull. Began burning off the bottom of the Cargo Hold 4, water tight door to fit the curvature of the damaged deck. Fit-up of the elliptical box doubler for PE-45 was started, and work began templating the curvature of the hull.

Saturday, 14 February. Templated and fit up elliptical box patches PE-45 and PD-57, welding was completed on PD-57 iaw WPS-404-W. The PD-57I doubler plate was also converted to an elliptical box patch, fit up, and tacked in place. Carbon arc cutting of the starboard hull breach crack arrest holes was completed. Phoenix topside welders completed burning the bottom of the Cargo Hold 4 water tight door to fit the curvature of the damaged deck. Fractured weld seams PF-57 and PF-54 were contour ground.

Sunday, 15 February. An external traverse stiffener was installed on elliptical box patch PE-45. The patch was re-fit and tacked in place. Completed welding PE-45 iaw WPS-202-W and PD-57I iaw WPS-404-W. UWMT and UWVT was completed on PD-57, PD-57I, and PE-45, all results were acceptable. All known underwater repairs were completed.

Monday, 16 February. The Phoenix Diving Supervisor and NAVSEA Technical Representative attended a meeting with the Port Engineer to discuss the scope of internal repairs. Welding utilities and repair equipment was established near internal repair sites. Outboard Fixed Ballast Tank 4A was drilled and tapped to install a carbon dioxide inlet. The space was filled with carbon dioxide, and welding on external bulkheads were deemed safe for hot work. Completed a crack repair in the wing fuel tank at Frame 57A, repair ID PI-57A (36 inch linear fracture in a longitudinal weld seam between the Cargo Hold 4A deck and Wing Fuel Tank 4A inboard bulkhead). Installation of the bottom seal plate on the Cargo Hold 4A watertight door was completed. Interference was removed on a crack at Frame 57, repair ID PI-57 (14-inch linear fracture in a longitudinal weld seam between the Cargo Hold 4A deck and the Wing Fuel Tank 4A inboard bulkhead), Frame 52, repair ID PI-52 (47-inch linear fracture in a longitudinal weld seam between the deck and the outboard J-ballast tank), and on a long transverse crack at Frame 47, repair ID PI-47.

Tuesday, 17 February. The Phoenix Diving Supervisor and NAVSEA Technical Representative attended a meeting with the Port Engineer, Chief Engineer, and Marine Chemist concerning hot work and tank status. Outboard Fixed Ballast Tanks 4A and 3A were filled with carbon dioxide and deemed safe for hot work. Completed weld repairs to PI-57. D&DCMT and D&DCVT were also completed on PI-57, results were acceptable. Interference was removed iso repairs at PI-47 (repair area along transverse bulkhead at Frame 47). Welding of a collar plate around vertical stiffener on transverse bulkhead at PI-47 was completed.

Wednesday, 18 February. The Phoenix Diving Supervisor and NAVSEA Technical Representative attended a meeting with the Port Engineer, Chief Engineer, and Marine Chemist concerning hot work and tank status. Fresh diesel fuel was found in Outboard J-Ballast Tank 3. A gas free certification was obtained from the Marine Chemist after the diesel was cleaned up. Completed crack repair on the forward bulkhead inside Wing Fuel Tank 4A on new repair site PI-57O. Weld buildup repairs were completed on crack PI-52: Collar plate installation was continued on vertical stiffener at transverse bulkhead at Frame 47 (PI-47). Work began excavating micro-fractures in the tank top of Outboard J-Ballast Tank 4 (PI-57I). The dive station was secured. Work began preparing ATUWS for transport, and packing Phoenix repair equipment.

Thursday, 19 February. The Phoenix Diving Supervisor and NAVSEA Technical Representative attended a meeting with the Port Engineer, Chief Engineer, and Marine Chemist concerning hot work and tank status. A gas free certification was obtained from the marine chemist. Repair site PI-47 was divided in to three separate repair IDs PI-47-1, PI-47-2, PI-47-3. Installation of collar plates on PI-47-1 and PI-47-3 were completed. Phoenix welders also completed weld buildup repairs on PI-47-2 and PI-57I. Dive station breakdown was completed. The transverse bulkhead plate at Frame 57 (PI-57 corner repair) was installed along with the sump and manhole cover plate. Preparations to the deck under port Watertight Door 4A were completed. Work continued packing Phoenix repair equipment.

Friday, 20 February. The Phoenix Diving Supervisor and NAVSEA Technical Representative attended a meeting with the Port Engineer, Chief Engineer, and Marine Chemist concerning hot work and tank status. A gas free certification was obtained from the Marine Chemist. Welding was completed on PI-57 (Corner repair). The port Watertight Door 4A bottom plate was cut to the contour of the deck and lowered in place. Completed seal welding the door to the deck. D&DCMT and D&DCVT were completed on all remaining internal repair sites, results were acceptable. All internal repairs were completed, and work began removing Phoenix welding support equipment from the ship. The floating dive platform was returned to Port Operations and arrangements were made to transport ATUWS I back to Sasebo. Work continued packing Phoenix repair equipment.

Saturday, 21 February. Six Phoenix personnel departed Okinawa, Japan and returned to their respective facilities. The short operational report was submitted to NAVSEA and the ABS Inspector. Work was completed removing welding and support equipment from USNS Matej Kocak. Local vendors removed all subcontracted equipment from the pier. The ABS Inspector completed an inspection of all internal repair sites. All Phoenix shipped equipment was palletized and prepared for transport back to the United States. Inventory was completed and dehumidifiers were installed in ATUWS I.

Sunday, 22 February. One Phoenix employee departed Okinawa, Japan and returned to Honolulu, Hawaii. Fuel was removed from ATUWS I and final preparations were made for the system to be transported.

Monday, 23 February. Two Phoenix personnel departed Okinawa, Japan and returned to their respective facilities. All Phoenix repair equipment was picked up for transport back to the United States. ATUWS I was picked up and shipped back to its point of origin.

Tuesday, 24 February. The Phoenix Diving Supervisor departed Okinawa, Japan and returned to his facility.

3.0 PROBLEMS ENCOUNTERED, RESOLUTION, AND RECOMMENDATIONS

3.1.

Problem: It proved difficult to source local steel for repairs that carried mill test certificates and ABS approval. Certified material could only be sourced on mainland Japan or the United States. The cost to expedite shipping of steel from mainland Japan to Okinawa was excessive.

Resolution: It proved immensely cheaper for Phoenix personnel to hand check steel with mill test certificates when traveling to Okinawa, Japan from the United States.

Recommendation: On similar future projects, send an assortment of certified and approved steel with Phoenix repair equipment on the forward end of the job.